SALADS FOR ALL SEASONS

ISBN: 1-879234-15-7

Library of Congress Catalog No. 96-077581

Published by Dockery House, a division of Heritage Publishing, Inc., 1720 Regal Row, Suite 228, Dallas, Texas, 75235.
Phone: 214-630-4300

HERITAGE PUBLISHING

Publisher . . . . .Rodney L. Dockery
Editorial Director . . . . .Caleb Pirtle III
Executive Editor . . . . .Kenneth E. Lively
Staff Writer . . . . .Bob Perkins Jr.
Editorial Assistant .Leigh Ann Linney
Art Director . . . . .Janet Todd
Book Designer . . . . .Mary Catherine Kozusko
Production Editor .Marnie Burkett
Photographer . . . . .Mark V. Davis/Davis Studios
Food Stylist . . . . .Patricia Fly

Vice President Corporate Sales . . . . .W. T. (Tom) Barron

Printed by The Bidal Group: David Terrazas, president.

Manufactured in the United States of America.

First Printing

TABLE OF CONTENTS

APPETIZERS

MEATLESS-SIDES

MEATLESS ENTRÉES

POULTRY

PORK & BEEF

FRUITS & DESSERTS

A GUIDE TO HEALTHY EATING

In *Salads For All Seasons*, our aim at Wal-Mart is to provide our customers with great-tasting recipes that have been designed to help you prepare healthy foods for your family.

Just remember these simple guidelines:

- Eat a variety of foods.
- Maintain a healthy weight.
- Choose a diet low in fat, saturated fat and cholesterol.
- Choose a diet with plenty of vegetables, fruits and grain products.

We are all concerned with calories, the measure of energy supplied by the foods we eat and drink. And some foods, quite simply, are higher in calories than other foods.

For example, whole-wheat bread has only 60 calories, while a donut contains 245 calories.

A baked potato only has 100 calories; whereas, French fries have 320 calories.

An apple has a mere 80 calories. But a slice of apple pie has 405 calories.

Foods like bread, potatoes or spaghetti are not really fattening. However, what you add to them can make them extremely high in calories. For example, that baked potato with only 100 calories suddenly contains 200 calories if you add one tablespoon of butter. And the calorie count goes to 300 calories if you pack on that second tablespoon of butter.

Another concern everyone has is cholesterol, a fat-like substance that is found in foods from animals sources, such as meat, poultry, fish, egg yolks, milk and milk products.

There is no cholesterol at all found in fruits, vegetables, breads and cereals, nuts, seeds, or dry beans and peas.

It is obvious that your body does indeed need some cholesterol to maintain good health. However, your own body makes the cholesterol it needs. The foods you eat only affect how much cholesterol is in your blood.

Eating too much cholesterol and saturated fat—a kind of fat found mainly in foods from animals—raises blood cholesterol levels in most people. High blood cholesterol levels can increase the risk of heart disease.

It is a good idea to limit the amount of fat, saturated fat and cholesterol you eat. Salads are a good way to accomplish that.

Fruits and fruit salads are a great way to eat healthy and stay healthy.

Fruit has a lot going for it: flavor, few calories, vitamins, minerals and fiber. And most fruits contain vitamin C, which keeps your gums healthy, as well as helping your body heal wounds and cuts.

The fiber found in fruits helps keep your digestive tract healthy. Besides fruits, some other plant foods that provide fiber are vegetables, whole-grain breads, whole-grain cereals, dry beans, dry peas, nuts and seeds.

Vegetables found in salads also add texture, vitamins, minerals and fiber to your meals. Deep yellow vegetables like carrots and sweet potatoes are worthwhile sources of vitamins, which keep your skin healthy, as well as protecting against infection and helping your vision.

Dark green vegetables like broccoli, collards and spinach have vitamins A and C, B vitamins, iron, calcium and more.

Starchy vegetables like potatoes, corn and lima beans have B vitamins.

And other vegetables like beets, cabbage, green beans, green peppers and tomatoes have both vitamins A and C.

Vegetables can be served raw, boiled, steamed, baked or microwaved. And you can add to their flavor in a variety of ways:

- Sprinkle ground cloves over baked yams and acorn squash.
- Mix a little oregano with cooked cabbage.
- Add cooked chopped onion to cooked peas.
- Cook carrots with crushed pineapple or pineapple juice.

Grains—breads, cereals, rice and pasta—possess vitamins, minerals and fiber as well. They are low in fat, and you should choose some whole-grain foods every day. Many of our salads take advantage of the rice and pasta.

Just remember that whole-grain breads have more fiber than white breads, and you can find many kinds of whole-grain foods: whole-wheat breads, bran flake cereals, oatmeal, brown rice, corn tortillas and pop-corn, to name a few.

At Wal-Mart, we want you to eat right.

We want you to eat healthy.

Our cookbooks can show the way.

GAZPACHO SALAD

6 cups diced Great Value Tomatoes
16 ounces Sam's American Choice Thick 'n Chunky Salsa
1/4 cup red wine vinegar
1/4 cup chopped Great Value Frozen Onion
1/4 cup chopped green onion
1/4 cup chopped Great Value Frozen Green Bell Pepper
1 (4 ounce) can green chilies, chopped and drained
4 garlic cloves, finely minced
2 cups chopped cucumber (1/4" cubes)
1/2 teaspoon coriander
2 tablespoons dried basil
1/2 cup olive oil
Great Value Salt and Pepper to taste
Sam's American Choice Tortilla Chips

- In a large bowl, combine all ingredients except tortilla chips. Quantities of various ingredients may be varied according to taste.
- Chill; serve with tortilla chips.
- Serves 8.

Total Calories: 153.47 Total Fat(g): 3.16 Sat. Fat(g): 0 Mono Fat(g): 1.72 Poly Fat(g): 13.78 Animal Fat(g): 0 Plant Fat(g): 3.16 Fish Fat(g): 0 Total Carb(g): 30.03 Comp. Carb(g): 29.91 Sugar(g): 0.12 Total Protein(g): 6.51 Anl Protein(g): 0 Plt Protein(g): 6.51 Fiber(g): 14.26 Chol(mg): 0 Sodium(mg): 1106.06 Potm(mg): 1529.02 Vitamin A: 314.7 Vitamin C(mg): 74.12 Iron(mg): 5.07 Calc(mg): 126.44 Phos(mg): 202.39 Alch(mg): 0 Caff(mg): 0 Asp(mg): 0 Water(g): 752.16 % of calories from fat: 18.53 (Nutritional information does not includes tortilla chips.)

ANTIPASTO SALAD AND MUSHROOM PESTO

8-10	*artichoke heart halves*
8-10	*Great Value Whole Tomatoes, sliced*
8-10	*Italian sweet peppers*
1	*cup sliced Great Value Black Olives*
8	*ounces Great Value Mushrooms*
1/2	*pound Great Value Mozzarella Cheese, cubed*
1/2	*cup chopped Great Value Frozen Onion*
	Great Value Parmesan Cheese, grated
	Crusty French bread

Dressing:

1	*cup Great Value Italian Salad Dressing*
4	*ounces wild mushroom pesto*
1	*tablespoon roasted garlic essence*

- In a large bowl, whisk the ingredients for the dressing.
- Add all the other ingredients.
- Toss and allow to marinate for 2 hours.
- Serve on a large platter.
- Sprinkle with grated Parmesan cheese. Serve with crusty French bread.
- Serves 8.

Total Calories: 298.22 Total Fat(g): 20.1 Sat. Fat(g): 0 Mono Fat(g): 10.23 Poly Fat(g): 3.84 Animal Fat(g): 9.44 Plant Fat(g): 10.66 Fish Fat(g): 0 Total Carb(g): 20.03 Comp. Carb(g): 19.81 Sugar(g): 0.22 Total Protein(g): 13.78 Anl Protein(g): 9.59 Plt Protein(g): 4.18 Fiber(g): 5.45 Chol(mg): 31.67 Sodium(mg): 506.82 Potm(mg): 704.87 Vitamin A: 263.18 Vitamin C(mg): 110.21 Iron(mg): 2.38 Calc(mg): 329.92 Phos(mg): 293.63 Alch(mg): 0 Caff(mg): 0 Asp(mg): 0 Water(g): 291.66 % of calories from fat: 60.66 (Nutritional information does not include bread.)

RANCH STYLE ANTIPASTO SALAD

- 1 *cup Great Value Diced Tomatoes*
- 1 *cup sliced Great Value Black Olives*
- 1 *cup sliced Great Value Mushrooms*
- 1 *large green bell pepper, julienned*
- 1 *large sweet red pepper, julienned*
- 1 *large yellow bell pepper, julienned*
- 4 *ounces Great Value Monterey Jack Cheese, cut into strips*
- 4 *ounces Great Value Cheddar Cheese, cut into strips*
- 8 *ounces Great Value Smoked Sausage, cut into strips*

Dressing:

- 1/4 *cup Great Value Vinegar*
- 1/3 *cup Great Value Vegetable Oil*
- 1/4 *cup water*
- 2 *tablespoons Great Value Sugar*
- 1 *cup Sam's American Choice Thick 'n Chunky Salsa*

- Mix all dressing ingredients together; let stand 10 minutes.
- Pour dressing over combined vegetables.
- Cover; marinate in refrigerator.
- Drain; arrange vegetables on platter.
- Serve with reserved marinade.
- Serves 6.

Total Calories: 250.14 Total Fat(g): 16.91 Sat. Fat(g): 0 Mono Fat(g): 7.73 Poly Fat(g): 1.66 Animal Fat(g): 11.68 Plant Fat(g): 4.97 Fish Fat(g): 0 Total Carb(g): 14.45 Comp. Carb(g): 10.3 Sugar(g): 4.15 Total Protein(g): 9.83 Anl Protein(g): 8.48 Plt Protein(g): 1.35 Fiber(g): 6.68 Chol(mg): 34.57 Sodium(mg): 884.34 Potm(mg): 439.76 Vitamin A: 282.04 Vitamin C(mg): 111.84 Iron(mg): 2.63 Calc(mg): 259.46 Phos(mg): 208.76 Alch(mg): 0 Caff(mg): 0 Asp(mg): 0 Water(g): 121.57 % of calories from fat: 60.84

BROCCOLI-CAULIFLOWER MARINADE

1	*(16 ounce) package Great Value Frozen Cauliflower, cut or broken into small flowerettes*
1	*(16 ounce) package Great Value Frozen Broccoli, cut or broken into small flowerettes*
1	*small cucumber, sliced*
1	*small green pepper, cut into strips*
1/2	*cup chopped Great Value Onion*
2	*cups (wedges) Great Value Tomatoes*
1	*cup sliced Great Value Black Olives*
1	*(16 ounce) bottle Great Value Italian Dressing*
	Great Value Salt and Pepper to taste

- Toss vegetables to mix.
- Pour Italian dressing over them and toss lightly until all pieces are covered, seasoning with salt and pepper to taste.
- Place in refrigerator in a covered dish, marinating 8-12 hours.
- Toss once or twice while marinating.
- Serves 6.

Total Calories: 129.91 Total Fat(g): 6.83 Sat. Fat(g): 0 Mono Fat(g): 5.11 Poly Fat(g): 2.12 Animal Fat(g): 0 Plant Fat(g): 6.83 Fish Fat(g): 0 Total Carb(g): 15.26 Comp. Carb(g): 14.58 Sugar(g): 0.68 Total Protein(g): 4.18 Anl Protein(g): 0 Plt Protein(g): 4.18 Fiber(g): 6.77 Chol(mg): 0 Sodium(mg): 636.2 Potm(mg): 566.34 Vitamin A: 267.28 Vitamin C(mg): 105.31 Iron(mg): 2.06 Calc(mg): 85.25 Phos(mg): 106.42 Alch(mg): 0 Caff(mg): 0 Asp(mg): 0 Water(g): 198.77 % of calories from fat: 47.32

MOZZARELLA AND TOMATO SALAD

1	*large Great Value Whole Tomato*
1/2	*pound Great Value Mozzarella Cheese*
	Boston lettuce leaves
	Great Value Salt and Pepper to taste
	Extra virgin olive oil
	Fresh basil leaves, torn or cut into small pieces

- Slice tomatoes and mozzarella into uniform slices, approximately 1/4" thick.
- Arrange slices alternately on a platter or individual salad plates atop lettuce leaves.
- Sprinkle with salt and pepper to taste.
- Drizzle with olive oil and sprinkle with fresh basil.
- Serves 2.

Total Calories: 574.73 Total Fat(g): 52.94 Sat. Fat(g): 0 Mono Fat(g): 27.51 Poly Fat(g): 3.96 Animal Fat(g): 24.69 Plant Fat(g): 28.23 Fish Fat(g): 0 Total Carb(g): 5.91 Comp. Carb(g): 5.66 Sugar(g): 0.25 Total Protein(g): 22.51 Anl Protein(g): 21.86 Plt Protein(g): 0.64 Fiber(g): 1.03 Chol(mg): 89.06 Sodium(mg): 1011.09 Potm(mg): 239.54 Vitamin A: 321.23 Vitamin C(mg): 12.69 Iron(mg): 0.83 Calc(mg): 596.16 Phos(mg): 438.86 Alch(mg): 0 Caff(mg): 0 Asp(mg): 0 Water(g): 127.61 % of calories from fat: 82.9

CONFETTI ASPARAGUS TOSS

- 1 *pound fresh asparagus, cut in 2" slices*
- 1 *small head lettuce, torn in bite-size pieces*
- 1 *cup thinly sliced celery*
- 1/4 *cup chopped Great Value Frozen Onion*
- 1/4 *cup Great Value Vegetable Oil*
- 2 *tablespoons Great Value White Wine Vinegar*
- 2 *tablespoons Great Value Lemon Juice*
- 1/4 *cup finely chopped Great Value Beets*
- 1 *hard boiled egg, finely chopped*
- 1 *tablespoon snipped parsley*
- 1 *teaspoon paprika*
- 1 *teaspoon Great Value Sugar*
- 1 *teaspoon Great Value Salt*
- 1/2 *teaspoon dry mustard*
- 4 *drops hot pepper sauce*

- Cook asparagus until tender; drain and chill.
- Combine with lettuce, celery and onion.
- For dressing, combine remaining ingredients in a jar; cover and shake well.
- Pour dressing over salad; toss lightly.
- Serves 6.

Total Calories: 59.07 Total Fat(g): 0.48 Sat. Fat(g): 0 Mono Fat(g): 1 Poly Fat(g): 0.1 Animal Fat(g): 0.89 Plant Fat(g): 0.3 Fish Fat(g): 0 Total Carb(g): 8.2 Comp. Carb(g): 7.36 Sugar(g): 0.85 Total Protein(g): 2.33 Anl Protein(g): 1.06 Plt Protein(g): 2.33 Fiber(g): 1.91 Chol(mg): 35.76 Sodium(mg): 187.84 Potm(mg): 353.22 Vitamin A: 101.84 Vitamin C(mg): 13.64 Iron(mg): 1.5 Calc(mg): 47.85 Phos(mg): 74.32 Alch(mg): 0 Caff(mg): 0 Asp(mg): 0 Water(g): 192.69 % of calories from fat: 7.31

COPPER PENNIES

2	*(16 ounce) packages Great Value Frozen Crinkle Cut Carrots*
3/4	*cup chopped Great Value Green Bell Pepper*
1/2	*cup chopped Great Value Frozen Onion*
1/2	*cup sliced celery*

Dressing:

1/2	*(10.75 ounce) can Great Value Tomato Soup*
3/8	*cup Great Value Sugar*
1/2	*teaspoon Great Value Mustard*
1/2	*teaspoon Worcestershire Sauce*
1/4	*cup Great Value Vegetable Oil*
3/8	*cup Great Value Vinegar*
	Great Value Salt and Pepper to taste

- Boil crinkle cut carrots until just tender; drain well.
- Cool; add green pepper, onion and celery.
- For dressing, thoroughly blend all ingredients in a blender; refrigerate.
- Toss together vegetables and dressing.
- Serves 8.

Total Calories: 110.35 Total Fat(g): 1.69 Sat. Fat(g): 0 Mono Fat(g): 0.61 Poly Fat(g): 2.12 Animal Fat(g): 0 Plant Fat(g): 0.69 Fish Fat(g): 0.06 Total Carb(g): 18.43 Comp. Carb(g): 10.83 Sugar(g): 9.5 Total Protein(g): 1.67 Anl Protein(g): 0.06 Plt Protein(g): 1.67 Fiber(g): 4.43 Chol(mg): 0 Sodium(mg): 510.75 Potm(mg): 232.59 Vitamin A: 1966.79 Vitamin C(mg): 9.84 Iron(mg): 0.92 Calc(mg): 39.59 Phos(mg): 36.09 Alch(mg): 0 Caff(mg): 0 Asp(mg): 0 Water(g): 124.83 % of calories from fat: 7.73

CARROT AND RAISIN SALAD

6	*Great Value Frozen Carrots*
1/4	*cup chopped Great Value Frozen Onion*
1	*fresh ginger root*
1/3	*cup Great Value Raisins*
2	*tablespoons Sam's American Choice Orange Juice*
2	*tablespoons brandy*
1	*tablespoon raspberry vinegar*
8	*ounces poppy seed dressing*

- Grate carrots, onion and ginger root in food processor.
- Heat raisins, orange juice and brandy in a microwave on HIGH (or on the stove in a non-aluminum pan).
- Add plumped raisins, with liquid and raspberry vinegar, to carrot mixture.
- Add poppy seed dressing.
- Chill at least one hour before serving. Keeps 2 weeks in refrigerator.
- Serves 8.

Total Calories: 155.19 Total Fat(g): 6.78 Sat. Fat(g): .5 Mono Fat(g): 1.2 Poly Fat(g): 0.39 Animal Fat(g): 0 Plant Fat(g): 0.28 Fish Fat(g): 0 Total Carb(g): 17.71 Comp. Carb(g): 17.71 Sugar(g): 3 Total Protein(g): 1.32 Anl Protein(g): 0 Plt Protein(g): 1.32 Fiber(g): 2.15 Chol(mg): .5 Sodium(mg): 121.66 Potm(mg): 365.1 Vitamin A: 1550.03 Vitamin C(mg): 37 Iron(mg): 0.54 Calc(mg): 26.39 Phos(mg): 43.75 Alch(mg): 2.35 Caff(mg): 0 Asp(mg): 0 Water(g): 112.19 % of calories from fat: 2.79

CARROT PLUS THREE SALAD

3	*cups grated Great Value Frozen Carrots*
2	*unpeeled apples, chopped*
1/2	*cup Great Value Raisins*
1/4	*cup chopped Great Value Dry Roasted Peanuts*
1	*cup Great Value Plain Yogurt*
3	*tablespoons Great Value Salad Dressing*
1	*teaspoon Great Value Lemon Juice*
	Lettuce leaves

- Combine carrots, apples, raisins and peanuts in a salad bowl.
- Blend together remaining ingredients and add to carrot mixture.
- Serve on lettuce leaves.
- Serves 6.

Total Calories: 207.96 Total Fat(g): 7.69 Sat. Fat(g): 2 Mono Fat(g): 3.38 Poly Fat(g): 2.74 Animal Fat(g): 0.59 Plant Fat(g): 4.1 Fish Fat(g): 0 Total Carb(g): 26.15 Comp. Carb(g): 26.15 Sugar(g): 0 Total Protein(g): 4.71 Anl Protein(g): 2.01 Plt Protein(g): 2.7 Fiber(g): 3.57 Chol(mg): 2.33 Sodium(mg): 99.77 Potm(mg): 472.4 Vitamin A: 1581.34 Vitamin C(mg): 8.83 Iron(mg): 0.72 Calc(mg): 98.89 Phos(mg): 120.84 Alch(mg): 0 Caff(mg): 0 Asp(mg): 0 Water(g): 129.31 % of calories from fat: 28.53

ARTICHOKE HEARTS AND PECANS

2	*(#2) cans artichoke hearts, drained*
2	*tablespoons Great Value Butter*
2	*tablespoons Great Value Flour*
1	*cup cream*
	Great Value Salt and Pepper to taste
	Hot pepper sauce to taste
1/2	*cup broken pecans*
1/2	*cup Great Value Bread Crumbs*
2	*tablespoons grated Great Value Parmesan Cheese*

- Arrange artichoke hearts in small casserole.
- Blend butter and flour in a saucepan; add cream.
- Cook, stirring constantly, until thickened.
- Season to taste with salt, pepper and hot pepper sauce.
- Pour sauce over artichoke hearts; add pecans.
- Sprinkle with bread crumbs and cheese.
- Bake at 300 degrees until bubbly.
- Serves 6.

Total Calories: 190.12 Total Fat(g): 12.18 Sat. Fat(g): 0 Mono Fat(g): 5.62 Poly Fat(g): 2.1 Animal Fat(g): 6.27 Plant Fat(g): 6.58 Fish Fat(g): 0 Total Carb(g): 17.87 Comp. Carb(g): 17.7 Sugar(g): 0.17 Total Protein(g): 6.16 Anl Protein(g): 1.76 Plt Protein(g): 4.4 Fiber(g): 4.28 Chol(mg): 16.02 Sodium(mg): 858.55 Potm(mg): 273.07 Vitamin A: 63.45 Vitamin C(mg): 6.04 Iron(mg): 1.61 Calc(mg): 66.07 Phos(mg): 110.55 Alch(mg): 0 Caff(mg): 0 Asp(mg): 0 Water(g): 50.81 % of calories from fat: 57.66

PINTO BEAN COMBINATION SALAD

- 2 *cups cooked Great Value Pinto Beans*
- 1 *(6 ounce) package lemon or lime gelatin*
- 3 *teaspoons Great Value Vinegar*
- 1/2 *teaspoon Great Value Salt*
- 2 *dashes Accent*
- 1/4 *cup chopped pimiento*
- 1/4 *cup chopped Great Value Frozen Green Bell Pepper*
- 1 *teaspoon minced Great Value Frozen Onion*
- 2 *medium Great Value Whole Tomatoes, peeled and sliced*
- *Spinach leaves to garnish*
- *Stuffed Great Value Olives to garnish*
- *Great Value Salad Dressing to garnish*

- Prepare gelatin according to package directions, using vinegar as part of liquid; add salt and Accent. Set aside to cool.
- Place small piece of pimiento in center of individual molds or several pieces in bottom of mold.
- Add enough pinto beans to cover bottom.
- Sprinkle green pepper and onion over beans.
- Add remaining beans; top with tomato slices.
- Pour cooled gelatin mixture over ingredients until tomato slices are covered. Chill until firm.
- Unmold on spinach leaves and garnish with olives and salad dressing.
- Serves 4.

Total Calories: 162.33 Total Fat(g): 2.5 Sat. Fat(g): 0 Mono Fat(g): 0.34 Poly Fat(g): 1.82 Animal Fat(g): 0 Plant Fat(g): 2.5 Fish Fat(g): 0 Total Carb(g): 31.65 Comp. Carb(g): 26.79 Sugar(g): 4.86 Total Protein(g): 8.62 Anl Protein(g): 0.38 Plt Protein(g): 8.25 Fiber(g): 8.56 Chol(mg): 0.19 Sodium(mg): 311.36 Potm(mg): 587.55 Vitamin A: 80.67 Vitamin C(mg): 28.59 Iron(mg): 3.12 Calc(mg): 48.77 Phos(mg): 158.24 Alch(mg): 0 Caff(mg): 0 Asp(mg): 0 Water(g): 139.13 % of calories from fat: 13.86

COUNTRY PINTO BEAN SALAD

- 2 *cups cooked Great Value Pinto Beans*
- 1/2 *cup Great Value Tomato Sauce*
- 2 *tablespoons crumbled Great Value Cheddar Cheese*
- 1 *tablespoon minced Great Value Frozen Onion*
- 1 *tablespoon Great Value Mustard*
- 1/4 *cup chopped Great Value Frozen Green Bell Pepper*
- 1/4 *cup minced celery*
- 1 *tablespoon Worcestershire Sauce*
- 1 *tablespoon Great Value Vinegar*
- 6 *Great Value Whole Tomatoes*
- *Great Value Leaf Spinach*
- *Parsley or watercress to garnish*

- Mix all ingredients, except tomatoes, spinach and garnish; chill.
- Cut tomatoes in wedges. Place on spinach leaves; fill with chilled salad.
- Garnish with parsley or watercress.
- Serves 6.

Total Calories: 140.68 Total Fat(g): 3.31 Sat. Fat(g): 0 Mono Fat(g): 1.25 Poly Fat(g): 1.21 Animal Fat(g): 1.75 Plant Fat(g): 1.41 Fish Fat(g): 0.17 Total Carb(g): 23.32 Comp. Carb(g): 22.75 Sugar(g): 0.56 Total Protein(g): 7.89 Anl Protein(g): 1.59 Plt Protein(g): 6.47 Fiber(g): 7.01 Chol(mg): 6 Sodium(mg): 218.24 Potm(mg): 683.41 Vitamin A: 124.46 Vitamin C(mg): 31.55 Iron(mg): 2.7 Calc(mg): 83.6 Phos(mg): 163 Alch(mg): 0 Caff(mg): 0 Asp(mg): 0 Water(g): 191.97 % of calories from fat: 21.18

HONEY VEGETABLE SALAD

- 1 (16 ounce) can Great Value Cut Green Beans, drained
- 1 1/2 cups Great Value Kernel Corn
- 1 1/2 cups Great Value Field Peas
- 1 (16 ounce) can Great Value Kidney Beans, drained
- 1 cup diced celery
- 1 green pepper, sliced
- 1/2 cup chopped Great Value Frozen Onion
- Great Value Salt to taste
- Dash Great Value Pepper
- 1/3 cup soybean oil
- 1/2 cup Great Value Honey
- 1/4 teaspoon dry mustard
- 1/4 cup red wine vinegar
- 1 cup cubed Great Value Colby Cheese

- In a large bowl, combine vegetables, salt and pepper to taste.
- Place oil, honey, mustard and wine vinegar in a jar and shake to blend.
- Pour over vegetables.
- Cover and refrigerate overnight.
- Sprinkle cheese cubes over top of salad to serve.
- Serves 8.

Total Calories: 357.19 Total Fat(g): 21.86 Sat. Fat(g): 0 Mono Fat(g): 11.34 Poly Fat(g): 2.41 Animal Fat(g): 14.12 Plant Fat(g): 7.73 Fish Fat(g): 0 Total Carb(g): 20.03 Comp. Carb(g): 19.78 Sugar(g): 0.25 Total Protein(g): 24.2 Anl Protein(g): 18.89 Plt Protein(g): 5.32 Fiber(g): 6.27 Chol(mg): 66.48 Sodium(mg): 992.8 Potm(mg): 881.12 Vitamin A: 178.87 Vitamin C(mg): 15.03 Iron(mg): 4.01 Calc(mg): 54.24 Phos(mg): 235.88 Alch(mg): 0 Caff(mg): 0 Asp(mg): 0 Water(g): 184.81 % of calories from fat: 55.08

CREAMY NEW POTATO SALAD

1	*cup Great Value Lite Yogurt*
1	*cup Great Value Honey Dijon Ranch Salad Dressing*
1	*tablespoon Sam's American Choice Dijon Mustard*
1/4	*cup dried dill weed*
8	*cups quartered Great Value Whole Potatoes, boiled and cooled*
1	*cup diced green pepper*
1	*cup chopped Great Value Red Onion*
1	*cup sliced celery*
	Great Value Salt and Pepper to taste

- In a large bowl, combine lite yogurt and salad dressing with Dijon mustard and dill weed.
- Add potatoes, green pepper, red onion and celery. Toss to combine.
- Add salt and pepper to taste.
- Cover and chill well.
- Serves 8.

Total Calories: 164.45 Total Fat(g): 2.87 Sat. Fat(g): 0 Mono Fat(g): 2.85 Poly Fat(g): 2.47 Animal Fat(g): 0.08 Plant Fat(g): 2.78 Fish Fat(g): 0 Total Carb(g): 34.19 Comp. Carb(g): 34.18 Sugar(g): 0.16 Total Protein(g): 5.02 Anl Protein(g): 1.75 Plt Protein(g): 3.39 Fiber(g): 4.95 Chol(mg): 1.78 Sodium(mg): 369.76 Potm(mg): 744.63 Vitamin A: 10.53 Vitamin C(mg): 33.63 Iron(mg): 1.78 Calc(mg): 103.8 Phos(mg): 127.82 Alch(mg): 0 Caff(mg): 0 Asp(mg): 0 Water(g): 174.65 % of calories from fat: 15.71

GERMAN POTATO SALAD

1	*(14.5 ounce) can Great Value Red Potatoes, drained*
1	*teaspoon Great Value Sugar*
1/2	*teaspoon Great Value Salt*
1/4	*teaspoon dry mustard*
1/8	*teaspoon Great Value Pepper*
2	*tablespoons white wine vinegar*
1	*cup Great Value Sour Cream*
1/2	*cup sliced cucumbers*
	Paprika

- Slice potatoes.
- Mix sugar, salt, mustard, pepper and vinegar.
- Add sour cream and cucumber; mix.
- Pour over potatoes and toss lightly.
- Before serving, sprinkle with paprika.
- Serve warm or cold.
- Serves 4.

Total Calories: 212.55 Total Fat(g): 11 Sat. Fat(g): 0 Mono Fat(g): 3.67 Poly Fat(g): 6.56 Animal Fat(g): 10.12 Plant Fat(g): 0.89 Fish Fat(g): 0 Total Carb(g): 25.45 Comp. Carb(g): 24.33 Sugar(g): 1.13 Total Protein(g): 6.21 Anl Protein(g): 1.62 Plt Protein(g): 4.59 Fiber(g): 5.04 Chol(mg): 21.66 Sodium(mg): 780.26 Potm(mg): 906.72 Vitamin A: 168.98 Vitamin C(mg): 36.35 Iron(mg): 2.58 Calc(mg): 148.91 Phos(mg): 141.24 Alch(mg): 0 Caff(mg): 0 Asp(mg): 0 Water(g): 478.89 % of calories from fat: 46.58

BAKED POTATO SALAD

1/2	*cup Sam's American Choice Honey Dijon Ranch Salad Dressing*
1	*cup sliced asparagus (lightly cooked or raw)*
1 1/2	*cups Great Value Frozen Broccoli Spears*
1	*cup Great Value Mushrooms*
1/2	*cup chopped Great Value Frozen Green Bell Pepper*
4	*baking potatoes*
1/4	*cup grated Great Value Sharp Cheddar Cheese*
	Lettuce leaves
	Great Value Black Olives and Great Value Gherkins, chopped to garnish

- Pour salad dressing over asparagus, broccoli, mushrooms and peppers.
- Cover and marinate in refrigerator several hours.
- Bake potatoes and split open.
- Top baked potato with vegetable mixture and Cheddar cheese.
- Serve on lettuce leaves.
- Garnish with black olives and gherkins.
- Serves 4.

Total Calories: 334.73 Total Fat(g): 6.58 Sat. Fat(g): 0 Mono Fat(g): 3.84 Poly Fat(g): 1.96 Animal Fat(g): 2.64 Plant Fat(g): 3.73 Fish Fat(g): 0 Total Carb(g): 64.01 Comp. Carb(g): 59.51 Sugar(g): 4.57 Total Protein(g): 11.3 Anl Protein(g): 2.18 Plt Protein(g): 9.18 Fiber(g): 9.02 Chol(mg): 9.64 Sodium(mg): 274.07 Potm(mg): 1182.01 Vitamin A: 197.34 Vitamin C(mg): 63.54 Iron(mg): 4.26 Calc(mg): 142.18 Phos(mg): 247.6 Alch(mg): 0 Caff(mg): 0 Asp(mg): 0 Water(g): 277.77 % of calories from fat: 17.69

SOUTH OF THE BORDER MARINATED VEGETABLES

1	*(16 ounce) package Great Value Frozen Cauliflower, broken into flowerettes*
1	*(16 ounce) package Great Value Frozen Broccoli, broken into flowerettes*
1	*cup diced Great Value Frozen Green Bell Pepper*
1	*cup chopped Great Value Frozen Onion*
1	*(16 ounce) jar Great Value Salsa, mild or hot*
1	*cup Great Value White Vinegar*
1	*cup Great Value Sugar*
6	*whole cloves*
1	*teaspoon allspice*

- Blanch vegetables in boiling water for 5 minutes; drain.

- In a 2-quart saucepan over medium heat, combine salsa, vinegar, sugar, cloves and allspice.

- Bring to a boil; reduce heat and boil gently for 5 minutes.

- In clean, hot jars, alternate layers of broccoli, cauliflower, green pepper and onion, adding some of the marinade between each vegetable layer. Leave 1/2" head space at top of jar and seal.

- This vegetable marinade must be refrigerated.

- Yields four 8-ounce jars or three 15-ounce jars.

Total Calories: 213.93 Total Fat(g): 0.36 Sat. Fat(g): 0 Mono Fat(g): 2.66 Poly Fat(g): 0.56 Animal Fat(g): 0 Plant Fat(g): 0.36 Fish Fat(g): 0 Total Carb(g): 49.13 Comp. Carb(g): 16.75 Sugar(g): 32.38 Total Protein(g): 4.67 Anl Protein(g): 0 Plt Protein(g): 4.67 Fiber(g): 14.08 Chol(mg): 0 Sodium(mg): 969.01 Potm(mg): 680.82 Vitamin A: 293.62 Vitamin C(mg): 87.51 Iron(mg): 3.82 Calc(mg): 80.36 Phos(mg): 127.62 Alch(mg): 0 Caff(mg): 0 Asp(mg): 0 Water(g): 194.77 % of calories from fat: 1.51

OLD FASHIONED CORNBREAD SALAD

2	*(6 ounce) packages cornbread mix*
1/2	*cup finely chopped Great Value Frozen Green Bell Pepper*
1/2	*cup finely chopped Great Value Onion*
1	*Great Value Tomato, finely chopped*
1	*cup Great Value Whole Kernel Corn, drained*
3	*hard boiled eggs, chopped*
1/4	*teaspoon Great Value Salt*
2	*cups Great Value Ranch Salad Dressing*
2	*cups cubed Great Value Cooked Honey Ham*

- Bake cornbread according to directions, then cool and crumble.
- Mix all ingredients together and chill at least 2 hours for flavors to blend.
- Serves 15.

Total Calories: 189.8 Total Fat(g): 7.47 Sat. Fat(g): 2 Mono Fat(g): 1.91 Poly Fat(g): 1.06 Animal Fat(g): 3.26 Plant Fat(g): 1.21 Fish Fat(g): 0 Total Carb(g): 4.59 Comp. Carb(g): 3.37 Sugar(g): 3.5 Total Protein(g): 10.07 Anl Protein(g): 9.61 Plt Protein(g): 0.59 Fiber(g): 0.46 Chol(mg): 68 Sodium(mg): 730.23 Potm(mg): 198.92 Vitamin A: 26.05 Vitamin C(mg): 6.02 Iron(mg): 0.88 Calc(mg): 10.54 Phos(mg): 150.05 Alch(mg): 0 Caff(mg): 0 Asp(mg): 0 Water(g): 31.79 % of calories from fat: 44.8

MACARONI SALAD

- 1 *(7.25 ounce) package Great Value Macaroni and Cheese*
- 1/2 *cup chopped Great Value Frozen Onion*
- 1 *cup condensed milk*
- 2 *tablespoons Great Value Brown Mustard*
- 1/2 *cup sliced celery*
- 1/4 *cup Great Value Sweet Pickle Relish*
- 1/4 *cup Great Value Mayonnaise*

- Cook macaroni according to package directions; drain.
- Add onion, condensed milk, mustard and cheese sauce from macaroni dinner.
- Cool.
- Add remaining ingredients; toss lightly.
- Cool, then chill.
- Serves 4.

Total Calories: 345.64 Total Fat(g): 13.77 Sat. Fat(g): 1.25 Mono Fat(g): 3.86 Poly Fat(g): 7.84 Animal Fat(g): 1.43 Plant Fat(g): 10.98 Fish Fat(g): 0 Total Carb(g): 11.42 Comp. Carb(g): 3.75 Sugar(g): 7.67 Total Protein(g): 0.83 Anl Protein(g): 0.38 Plt Protein(g): 0.45 Fiber(g): 1.32 Chol(mg): 6.69 Sodium(mg): 239.25 Potm(mg): 109.28 Vitamin A: 9.37 Vitamin C(mg): 3.72 Iron(mg): 1.79 Calc(mg): 26.25 Phos(mg): 29.4 Alch(mg): 0 Caff(mg): 0 Asp(mg): 0 Water(g): 49.53 % of calories from fat: 74.8

PASTA PRIMAVERA SALAD

- 1/2 *pound Great Value Elbow Macaroni*
- 1/2 *pound Sam's American Choice Penne Rigate or Great Value Egg Noodles*
- 1 *cup Great Value Frozen Broccoli Flowerettes*
- 1/4 *cup olive oil*
- 1/2 *cup Great Value Whole Tomato (wedges)*
- 1/2 *cup chopped Great Value Frozen Onion*
- 1/2 *cup thinly sliced zucchini halves*
- 1/2 *cup diced celery*
- 1/2 *cup finely shredded red cabbage*
- 1/4 *cup julienned pickled red pepper*
- 1/4 *cup julienned green pepper*
- 1/4 *cup chopped parsley*
- 1/4 *cup shredded Great Value Carrots*
- 1/2 *teaspoon Great Value Salt*
- 1/4 *teaspoon Great Value Pepper*
- 1/8 *cup Great Value Lemon Juice*

- Bring to boil 4-5 quarts of water in a 6-8 quart pot.
- Drop elbow macaroni and penne rigate (or egg noodles) in water, stirring quickly for 10 seconds. Cook until al dente (approximately 3 minutes).
- Add the broccoli flowerettes and cook for another 30 seconds.
- Drain, rinse in cold water (to stop the cooking of the pasta) and drain again.
- Place the pasta in a large bowl, add the extra virgin olive oil and toss.
- Add all the vegetables, salt and pepper, and toss lightly again.
- Add the lemon juice and toss again.
- Serves 8. (Salad may be prepared ahead of time.)

Total Calories: 133.77 Total Fat(g): 1.06 Sat. Fat(g): 0 Mono Fat(g): 1.2 Poly Fat(g): 0.7 Animal Fat(g): 0.3 Plant Fat(g): 0.76 Fish Fat(g): 0 Total Carb(g): 26.13 Comp. Carb(g): 24.73 Sugar(g): 1.4 Total Protein(g): 5.09 Anl Protein(g): 0.43 Plt Protein(g): 4.68 Fiber(g): 2.53 Chol(mg): 14.27 Sodium(mg): 275.23 Potm(mg): 167.94 Vitamin A: 146.72 Vitamin C(mg): 18.05 Iron(mg): 1.46 Calc(mg): 28.18 Phos(mg): 73.28 Alch(mg): 0 Caff(mg): 0 Asp(mg): 0 Water(g): 122.44 % of calories from fat: 7.13

garlic
sweet basil
tomato
garlic
basil

PISTACHIO MACARONI SALAD

1/2 pound Sam's American Choice Rotini
2 cups torn Great Value Leaf Spinach
1 cup diced Great Value Tomato
1 cup Great Value Sweet Peas, drained
1/4 cup Great Value Pistachios
Great Value Pepper to taste
Great Value Parmesan Cheese, grated

Dressing:

1/4 cup Great Value Vegetable Oil
1/4 cup red wine vinegar
3/4 teaspoon crushed oregano
1/8 teaspoon garlic powder

- Combine dressing ingredients; set aside.
- Prepare rotini according to package directions; drain.
- Marinate hot rotini in dressing; cool to room temperature.
- Combine with spinach, tomato, peas, pistachios and pepper to taste.
- Sprinkle with Parmesan cheese.
- Serves 8.

Total Calories: 113.74 Total Fat(g): 3.98 Sat. Fat(g): 0 Mono Fat(g): 2.28 Poly Fat(g): 1.71 Animal Fat(g): 0.76 Plant Fat(g): 3.22 Fish Fat(g): 0 Total Carb(g): 15.03 Comp. Carb(g): 14.33 Sugar(g): 0.68 Total Protein(g): 5.08 Anl Protein(g): 1.06 Plt Protein(g): 4.02 Fiber(g): 2.68 Chol(mg): 1.97 Sodium(mg): 144.7 Potm(mg): 244.28 Vitamin A: 132.41 Vitamin C(mg): 10.98 Iron(mg): 1.39 Calc(mg): 60.22 Phos(mg): 87.12 Alch(mg): 0 Caff(mg): 0 Asp(mg): 0 Water(g): 52.37 % of calories from fat: 31.49

PASTA AND BEAN SALAD

- 1/2 *pound Great Value Elbow Macaroni, cooked and drained*
- 1 *(6 ounce) jar artichoke hearts, drained*
- 1 *(10.5 ounce) can Great Value Peas, drained*
- 1 *(10.5 ounce) can Great Value Red Kidney Beans, drained*
- 2 *stalks celery, sliced*
- 2 *Great Value Tomatoes, cut in wedges*

Dressing:

- 1/3 *cup olive oil*
- 3 *tablespoons red wine vinegar*
- 3/4 *teaspoon Italian seasoning*
- 1/4 *teaspoon dry mustard*
- 1/4 *teaspoon Great Value Pepper*
- 1/4 *teaspoon Great Value Sugar*
- 1/8 *teaspoon cayenne pepper*
- 1 *clove garlic, crushed*
- 1/4 *cup grated Great Value Parmesan Cheese*

- In a blender, combine ingredients for dressing; set aside.
- In a large bowl, combine remaining ingredients.
- Pour reserved dressing over salad and toss gently.
- Refrigerate 2 hours or overnight.
- Serves 6.

Total Calories: 254.27 Total Fat(g): 3.19 Sat. Fat(g): 0 Mono Fat(g): 2.1 Poly Fat(g): 1.79 Animal Fat(g): 1.01 Plant Fat(g): 2.18 Fish Fat(g): 0 Total Carb(g): 45.27 Comp. Carb(g): 45.13 Sugar(g): 0.27 Total Protein(g): 13.5 Anl Protein(g): 1.42 Plt Protein(g): 12.08 Fiber(g): 11.38 Chol(mg): 2.63 Sodium(mg): 1005.86 Potm(mg): 730.53 Vitamin A: 40.65 Vitamin C(mg): 13.79 Iron(mg): 4.11 Calc(mg): 124.38 Phos(mg): 249.13 Alch(mg): 0 Caff(mg): 0 Asp(mg): 0 Water(g): 239.76 % of calories from fat: 11.29

BLACK-EYED PEA SALAD OR DIP

1	*(16 ounce) package Great Value Black-eyed Peas*
1	*(14.5 ounce) can hominy with red and green peppers*
1/2	*cup chopped Great Value Frozen Onion*
1	*Great Value Frozen Green Bell Pepper, chopped*
2	*Great Value Tomatoes, coarsely chopped*
1	*clove garlic, minced*
1/2	*cup parsley*
3	*jalapeño chilies, minced*
1/3	*cup Great Value Vegetable Oil*
3	*tablespoons Great Value White Vinegar*
1/2	*teaspoon Great Value Salt*
2	*tablespoons chopped cilantro*
	Sam's American Choice Tortilla Chips

- Cook black-eyed peas according to package instructions until tender. Drain; cover with cold water. Drain well.
- In large bowl, combine peas with drained hominy and remaining ingredients. Cover and chill 2 hours or overnight, stirring occasionally.
- Serves 8 as a salad, or more as dip with Sam's American Choice Tortilla Chips.

Total Calories: 150.04 Total Fat(g): 4.58 Sat. Fat(g): 0 Mono Fat(g): 0.6 Poly Fat(g): 1.15 Animal Fat(g): 0 Plant Fat(g): 4.58 Fish Fat(g): 0 Total Carb(g): 9.45 Comp. Carb(g): 9.39 Sugar(g): 0.06 Total Protein(g): 1.44 Anl Protein(g): 0 Plt Protein(g): 1.44 Fiber(g): 3.83 Chol(mg): 0 Sodium(mg): 236.16 Potm(mg): 127.8 Vitamin A: 36.36 Vitamin C(mg): 26.49 Iron(mg): 0.62 Calc(mg): 10.65 Phos(mg): 29.96 Alch(mg): 0 Caff(mg): 0 Asp(mg): 0 Water(g): 86.86 % of calories from fat: 28.42 (Nutritional information does not include tortilla chips.)

RICE SALAD OLÉ

1	*cup cooked Great Value Long Grain Rice*
2	*tablespoons olive oil*
3	*tablespoons Great Value White Vinegar*
1	*teaspoon Great Value Salt*
1	*teaspoon Great Value Pepper*
1/2	*teaspoon tarragon*
1/4	*cup chopped Great Value Frozen Green Bell Pepper*
1/4	*cup chopped parsley*
1/4	*cup chopped chives*
1	*cup sliced Great Value Kosher Baby Dills*
	Lettuce leaves
	Hard boiled eggs and pimiento to garnish

- Mix rice with olive oil, vinegar, salt, pepper and tarragon.
- Cool; mix green pepper, parsley, chives and kosher baby dills.
- Serve on lettuce leaves. Garnish with hard boiled eggs and pimiento.
- Serves 3.

Total Calories: 332.55 Total Fat(g): 21.37 Sat. Fat(g): 0 Mono Fat(g): 11.37 Poly Fat(g): 4.8 Animal Fat(g): 5.36 Plant Fat(g): 16.01 Fish Fat(g): 0 Total Carb(g): 43.33 Comp. Carb(g): 42.5 Sugar(g): 0.84 Total Protein(g): 14.26 Anl Protein(g): 6.38 Plt Protein(g): 7.88 Fiber(g): 1.73 Chol(mg): 214.54 Sodium(mg): 1514.27 Potm(mg): 199.91 Vitamin A: 127.15 Vitamin C(mg): 15.52 Iron(mg): 3.78 Calc(mg): 56.06 Phos(mg): 144.25 Alch(mg): 0 Caff(mg): 0 Asp(mg): 0 Water(g): 60.28 % of calories from fat: 57.83

SUMMER ROTINI SALAD

2 packages Great Value Rotini
1 jar marinated artichoke hearts
1 (15 ounce) can Great Value Kidney Beans, drained
1 (6 ounce) can Great Value Black Olives, chopped or sliced
5 ounces stuffed Great Value Green Olives
1 jar roasted red peppers in oil
1 cup diced Great Value Mozzarella Cheese
1 cup diced Great Value Cheddar Cheese
1 cup diced Great Value Cooked Smoked Turkey
1 (12 ounce) bottle Great Value Italian Salad Dressing

- Cook rotini according to package directions; drain, rinse with cold water and set aside.
- Combine remaining ingredients, except Italian salad dressing.
- Add rotini to mixture and toss with Italian dressing.
- Chill at least 4 hours before serving.
- Serves 8.

Total Calories: 524.61 Total Fat(g): 17.58 Sat. Fat(g): 0 Mono Fat(g): 8.78 Poly Fat(g): 0 Animal Fat(g): 14.59 Plant Fat(g): 2.38 Fish Fat(g): 0 Total Carb(g): 61.72 Comp. Carb(g): 62.86 Sugar(g): 1.14 Total Protein(g): 30.21 Anl Protein(g): 16.68 Plt Protein(g): 13.54 Fiber(g): 7.76 Chol(mg): 60.46 Sodium(mg): 671.82 Potm(mg): 524.42 Vitamin A: 224.84 Vitamin C(mg): 34.47 Iron(mg): 3.95 Calc(mg): 381.98 Phos(mg): 460.63 Alch(mg): 0 Caff(mg): 0 Asp(mg): 0 Water(g): 120.94 % of calories from fat: 30.16

COUNTRY CHICKEN AND PASTA SALAD

1	*(8 ounce) package Great Value Elbow Macaroni*
1/2	*pound Great Value Chicken Breast Tenderloins*
1/2	*cup chopped Great Value Frozen Onion*
1/2	*cup sliced Great Value Olives*
1/4	*cup minced parsley*
6	*Great Value Tomatoes, quartered*
1/2	*cup Great Value Italian Salad Dressing*
	Spinach leaves to garnish

- Cook macaroni according to package directions.
- Bake chicken breast tenderloins according to package directions and thinly slice into strips.
- Combine all ingredients in a large bowl.
- Toss gently to coat with salad dressing.
- Cover and chill 3-4 hours or overnight.
- Serve as a cool main dish on a bed of spinach leaves.
- Serves 6.

Total Calories: 195.54 Total Fat(g): 5.59 Sat. Fat(g): 0 Mono Fat(g): 2.44 Poly Fat(g): 2.24 Animal Fat(g): 1.56 Plant Fat(g): 4.02 Fish Fat(g): 0 Total Carb(g): 21.27 Comp. Carb(g): 21.14 Sugar(g): 0.13 Total Protein(g): 17.33 Anl Protein(g): 13.51 Plt Protein(g): 3.82 Fiber(g): 2.46 Chol(mg): 36.99 Sodium(mg): 226.05 Potm(mg): 480.2 Vitamin A: 100.73 Vitamin C(mg): 25.39 Iron(mg): 2.02 Calc(mg): 36.8 Phos(mg): 166.61 Alch(mg): 0 Caff(mg): 0 Asp(mg): 0 Water(g): 173.9 % of calories from fat: 25.73

CARIBBEAN PASTA SALAD

2-3	*Great Value Chicken Breast Fillets*
2	*cups Sam's American Choice Penne Rigate*
10	*Great Value Tomatoes, quartered*
1/4	*cup diced red onion*
1/4	*cup sliced Great Value Green Olives*
1/4	*cup Great Value Green Peas*
1	*stalk celery, diced*
1/4	*cup diced Great Value Frozen Green Bell Pepper*
1	*Great Value Frozen Carrot, grated*
2	*tablespoons grated Great Value Parmesan Cheese*
	Purple kale to garnish

Dressing:

2	*tablespoons cream of coconut*
4	*tablespoons Great Value Sour Cream*
4	*tablespoons juice from can Great Value Sliced Pineapple*
2	*tablespoons Great Value Lemon Juice*

- Poach chicken breasts; save the water for the penne rigate.
- Put penne rigate in boiling water; cook 8-9 minutes. Rinse under cold water.
- Dice chicken breasts.
- Toss penne rigate, chicken, vegetables and cheese in bowl.
- Mix dressing and pour over pasta mixture.
- Toss again, garnish and service.
- Serves 4.

Total Calories: 646.09 Total Fat(g): 12.94 Sat. Fat(g): 0 Mono Fat(g): 4.12 Poly Fat(g): 3.28 Animal Fat(g): 6.86 Plant Fat(g): 6.07 Fish Fat(g): 0 Total Carb(g): 101.14 Comp. Carb(g): 74.43 Sugar(g): 26.72 Total Protein(g): 35.13 Anl Protein(g): 23.44 Plt Protein(g): 11.67 Fiber(g): 7.52 Chol(mg): 119.94 Sodium(mg): 435.62 Potm(mg): 1182.56 Vitamin A: 762.11 Vitamin C(mg): 82.13 Iron(mg): 5.19 Calc(mg): 133.39 Phos(mg): 403.69 Alch(mg): 0 Caff(mg): 0 Asp(mg): 0 Water(g): 520.84 % of calories from fat: 18.03

CHICKEN ROTINI SALAD

1/2	*pound Sam's American Choice Rotini*
3	*cups chopped Great Value Chicken Breast Fillets*
1 1/2	*cups sliced celery*
1	*medium red bell pepper, chopped*
1	*cup Great Value Peas, drained*
1/4	*cup sliced Great Value Olives*
1/4	*cup chopped Great Value Frozen Onion*
3/4	*cup Great Value Italian Salad Dressing*
1/4	*cup Great Value Parmesan Cheese*
1/4	*teaspoon Great Value Pepper*

- Prepare rotini according to package directions; drain.
- Bake chicken breast fillets according to package directions; chop into small pieces.
- In a medium bowl, combine rotini and remaining ingredients; mix well.
- Cover; chill thoroughly.
- Toss gently before serving.
- Serves 7.

Total Calories: 226.86 Total Fat(g): 4.49 Sat. Fat(g): 0 Mono Fat(g): 2.58 Poly Fat(g): 2.32 Animal Fat(g): 2.21 Plant Fat(g): 2.28 Fish Fat(g): 0 Total Carb(g): 27.76 Comp. Carb(g): 26.82 Sugar(g): 0.94 Total Protein(g): 18.46 Anl Protein(g): 12.79 Plt Protein(g): 5.67 Fiber(g): 3.24 Chol(mg): 33.96 Sodium(mg): 208.19 Potm(mg): 316.94 Vitamin A: 94.31 Vitamin C(mg): 25.39 Iron(mg): 1.87 Calc(mg): 69.23 Phos(mg): 179.88 Alch(mg): 0 Caff(mg): 0 Asp(mg): 0 Water(g): 87.02 % of calories from fat: 17.81

VAQUERO GARDEN SALAD

- 1 (16 ounce) jar Great Value Salsa, divided
- 1 cup Great Value Sour Cream
- 3 cups cooked and shredded Great Value Chicken Breast
- 1/4 cup water
- 1 (1.25 ounce) package Great Value Taco Seasoning Mix
- 1 head lettuce, torn into bite-size pieces
- 3 cups chopped Great Value Broccoli
- 1 small red onion, thinly sliced and separated into rings
- 1 avocado, peeled, pitted and chopped
- 1 Great Value Carrot, shredded
- 1 cup diced Great Value Tomato
- 1 (4 ounce) can green chilies, drained
- 1 cup grated Great Value Cheddar Cheese
- Sam's American Choice Tortilla Chips, broken

- Combine 1 cup salsa and sour cream; refrigerate until ready to serve.
- In a large skillet, combine chicken, remaining salsa, water and taco seasoning mix.
- Bring to a boil, then simmer 15-20 minutes.
- In a large serving bowl, layer vegetables.
- Top with chicken mixture, chilies and cheese. Toss to combine.
- Top each salad with broken tortilla chips, salsa and sour cream dressing.
- Serves 8.

Total Calories: 315.26 Total Fat(g): 16.02 Sat. Fat(g): 0 Mono Fat(g): 6.94 Poly Fat(g): 1.81 Animal Fat(g): 11.81 Plant Fat(g): 3.84 Fish Fat(g): 0 Total Carb(g): 14.67 Comp. Carb(g): 14.66 Sugar(g): 0.03 Total Protein(g): 27.33 Anl Protein(g): 24.61 Plt Protein(g): 2.73 Fiber(g): 10.3 Chol(mg): 81.29 Sodium(mg): 991.64 Potm(mg): 955.58 Vitamin A: 426.6 Vitamin C(mg): 53.03 Iron(mg): 3.94 Calc(mg): 180.82 Phos(mg): 335.74 Alch(mg): 0 Caff(mg): 0 Asp(mg): 0 Water(g): 237.72 % of calories from fat: 45.73 (Nutritional information does not include tortilla chips.)

BARBECUE CHICKEN SALAD

- 1/2 pound Great Value Barbecued Breast Fillets, cooked and shredded
- 1/2 medium-size lettuce head, cut in bite-size pieces
- 1 cup diced Great Value Tomatoes
- 1/2 cup chopped Great Value Onion
- 1/2 cup chopped Great Value Frozen Green Bell Pepper
- 1/2 cup chopped red pepper
- 1 small cucumber, coarsely chopped
- 1/2 cup Great Value Black Olives
- Great Value Hickory Barbecue Sauce
- 1 cup cubed Great Value Cheddar Cheese
- 3/4 cup Great Value Italian Salad Dressing
- Oregano

- Prepare barbecued breast fillets according to package directions; shred.
- Combine first 10 ingredients together.
- Add salad dressing to taste and a dash of oregano.
- Toss and refrigerate until ready to serve.
- Serves 4.

Total Calories: 335.01 Total Fat(g): 18.47 Sat. Fat(g): 0 Mono Fat(g): 8.09 Poly Fat(g): 2.25 Animal Fat(g): 12.88 Plant Fat(g): 4.8 Fish Fat(g): 0 Total Carb(g): 11.09 Comp. Carb(g): 10.67 Sugar(g): 0.44 Total Protein(g): 31.11 Anl Protein(g): 28.76 Plt Protein(g): 2.35 Fiber(g): 3.45 Chol(mg): 91.51 Sodium(mg): 440.84 Potm(mg): 605.28 Vitamin A: 269.07 Vitamin C(mg): 52.2 Iron(mg): 2.16 Calc(mg): 309.67 Phos(mg): 379.98 Alch(mg): 0 Caff(mg): 0 Asp(mg): 0 Water(g): 280.56 % of calories from fat: 49.62

CURRIED CHICKEN SALAD

2 1/2	*cups diced Great Value Chicken Breast Tenderloins*
1	*cup cubed Great Value Pineapple*
1	*cup diced celery*
1/2	*cup diced water chestnuts*
1	*teaspoon curry powder*
1	*tablespoon tamari sauce*
1/2	*cup Great Value Mayonnaise*
1/4	*cup Great Value Sour Cream*
1/4	*cup pineapple ginger chutney*
1	*tablespoon Great Value Lemon Juice*
1	*head lettuce, shredded*
1/2	*cup Great Value Dry Roasted Peanuts*

- Bake chicken breast tenderloins according to package directions; dice.
- Mix chicken with pineapple, celery and water chestnuts.
- Dissolve curry powder in tamari sauce; combine with mayonnaise, sour cream, chutney and lemon juice.
- Mix chicken with dressing.
- Serve on lettuce.
- Sprinkle with peanuts.
- Serves 5.

Total Calories: 439.52 Total Fat(g): 31.74 Sat. Fat(g): 0 Mono Fat(g): 12.18 Poly Fat(g): 15.45 Animal Fat(g): 6.15 Plant Fat(g): 25.43 Fish Fat(g): 0 Total Carb(g): 17.21 Comp. Carb(g): 15.61 Sugar(g): 1.6 Total Protein(g): 27.63 Anl Protein(g): 21.94 Plt Protein(g): 5.69 Fiber(g): 4.06 Chol(mg): 71.61 Sodium(mg): 529.72 Potm(mg): 635.02 Vitamin A: 63.92 Vitamin C(mg): 14.8 Iron(mg): 3.89 Calc(mg): 69.42 Phos(mg): 263.55 Alch(mg): 0 Caff(mg): 0 Asp(mg): 0 Water(g): 224.72 % of calories from fat: 64.99

CHINESE CHICKEN SALAD

- 1 1/2 cups baked and chopped Great Value Chicken Breast Tenderloins
- 3 cups torn Great Value Leaf Spinach
- 1 (8 ounce) can water chestnuts, drained
- 1/4 cup chopped red cabbage
- 1 cup sliced asparagus (cooked or raw)
- 1/2 cup julienned Great Value Frozen Carrot
- 1/4 cup chopped Great Value Frozen Onion
- Chow mein noodles to garnish

Dressing:

- 3 1/2 tablespoons soy sauce
- 1 tablespoon Great Value Sugar
- 2 tablespoons Great Value Vegetable Oil
- 2 tablespoons rice vinegar
- 1/2 teaspoon garlic powder
- 1/2 teaspoon Great Value Pepper
- 1/2 teaspoon sesame oil

- Bake chicken breast tenderloins according to package directions.
- Toss salad ingredients together. Set aside.
- Mix dressing ingredients.
- Combine salad mixture and dressing mixture; toss.
- Top with chow mein noodles.
- Serves 4.

Total Calories: 297.95 Total Fat(g): 16.08 Sat. Fat(g): 0 Mono Fat(g): 6.19 Poly Fat(g): 11.32 Animal Fat(g): 1.57 Plant Fat(g): 14.5 Fish Fat(g): 0 Total Carb(g): 24.13 Comp. Carb(g): 21.09 Sugar(g): 3.04 Total Protein(g): 19.98 Anl Protein(g): 13.51 Plt Protein(g): 6.47 Fiber(g): 3.86 Chol(mg): 37.87 Sodium(mg): 1037.06 Potm(mg): 612.99 Vitamin A: 705.06 Vitamin C(mg): 22.41 Iron(mg): 3.83 Calc(mg): 71.86 Phos(mg): 207.12 Alch(mg): 0 Caff(mg): 0 Asp(mg): 0 Water(g): 137.79 % of calories from fat: 48.57

LAYERED MEXICAN TURKEY SALAD

- 1 pound Great Value Cooked Honey Turkey
- 1 (15 ounce) can Great Value Chili Beans
- 1/4 cup Great Value Salsa (additional salsa for dressing)
- 1/4 teaspoon garlic powder
- 1 teaspoon Great Value Chili Seasoning
- 1/4 teaspoon Great Value Pepper
- 2 cups lettuce pieces
- 2 cups coarsely broken Sam's American Choice Tortilla Chips
- 1 cup grated Great Value Cheddar Cheese
- 1 cup diced Great Value Tomatoes
- 1/4 cup sliced Great Value Olives

- Dice turkey into small pieces.
- Add beans, salsa, garlic powder, chili seasoning and pepper; heat until hot.
- Layer in a salad bowl or large platter in this order: lettuce, tortilla chips, hot turkey mixture, tomatoes and olives.
- Use additional salsa for salad dressing.
- Serves 6.

Total Calories: 335.35 Total Fat(g): 13.92 Sat. Fat(g): 0 Mono Fat(g): 4.82 Poly Fat(g): 3.3 Animal Fat(g): 10.28 Plant Fat(g): 4.07 Fish Fat(g): 0 Total Carb(g): 25.81 Comp. Carb(g): 25.47 Sugar(g): 0.34 Total Protein(g): 27.04 Anl Protein(g): 21.09 Plt Protein(g): 5.95 Fiber(g): 6.74 Chol(mg): 60.63 Sodium(mg): 1595.3 Potm(mg): 675.09 Vitamin A: 230.95 Vitamin C(mg): 12.1 Iron(mg): 3.62 Calc(mg): 196.46 Phos(mg): 406.5 Alch(mg): 0 Caff(mg): 0 Asp(mg): 0 Water(g): 172.57 % of calories from fat: 37.36

TURKEY SALAD WITH CURRY DRESSING

6	*ounces Great Value Cooked Turkey Breast, thinly sliced into 1/2" strips*
2	*cups torn Great Value Leaf Spinach*
1/4	*cup grated Great Value Carrot*
2	*tablespoons Great Value Raisins*

Dressing:

2	*tablespoons Great Value Lite Mayonnaise*
2	*tablespoons Great Value Light Plain Yogurt*
1/2	*teaspoon curry powder*
1	*teaspoon Great Value Lemon Juice*

- Bake turkey breast strips and place in medium bowl with leaf spinach and carrot.
- Toss salad lightly; sprinkle with raisins.
- Cover tightly; chill.
- Make dressing by combining mayonnaise, yogurt, curry powder and lemon juice.
- Cover dressing tightly; chill.
- To serve, pour dressing over turkey breast salad; toss.
- Serves 2.

Total Calories: 211.99 Total Fat(g): 7.09 Sat. Fat(g): 0 Mono Fat(g): 2.04 Poly Fat(g): 5.99 Animal Fat(g): 1.87 Plant Fat(g): 5.2 Fish Fat(g): 0 Total Carb(g): 14.72 Comp. Carb(g): 13.71 Sugar(g): 1.01 Total Protein(g): 23.69 Anl Protein(g): 21.52 Plt Protein(g): 2.18 Fiber(g): 2.52 Chol(mg): 36.56 Sodium(mg): 1398.84 Potm(mg): 760.22 Vitamin A: 777.93 Vitamin C(mg): 22.4 Iron(mg): 3.27 Calc(mg): 126.86 Phos(mg): 283.36 Alch(mg): 0 Caff(mg): 0 Asp(mg): 0 Water(g): 157.88 % of calories from fat: 30.1

CHICKEN PEANUT SALAD

5	*cups cooked and shredded Great Value Chicken Breast Fillets*
	Bean sprouts
2	*tablespoons chopped Great Value Frozen Onion*
1/2	*cup chopped Great Value Dry Roasted Peanuts*

Dressing:

3	*tablespoons Great Value Peanut Butter*
5	*tablespoons Great Value Vegetable Oil*
1/4	*cup soy sauce*
1/4	*cup Great Value Sugar*
4	*teaspoons Great Value Vinegar*
1	*tablespoon sesame oil concentrate*
1/2	*teaspoon cayenne*

- In a blender, whirl all dressing ingredients together and store in refrigerator until ready for use.
- Spread chicken on platter, over bean sprouts, if desired.
- Sprinkle onion and peanuts on top; drizzle dressing to cover.
- Serves 6.

Total Calories: 486.46 Total Fat(g): 28.56 Sat. Fat(g): 0 Mono Fat(g): 11.45 Poly Fat(g): 12.97 Animal Fat(g): 4.18 Plant Fat(g): 24.38 Fish Fat(g): 0 Total Carb(g): 15.84 Comp. Carb(g): 7.2 Sugar(g): 8.63 Total Protein(g): 42.8 Anl Protein(g): 36.03 Plt Protein(g): 6.77 Fiber(g): 2.4 Chol(mg): 98.68 Sodium(mg): 272.13 Potm(mg): 516.4 Vitamin A: 14.36 Vitamin C(mg): 6.09 Iron(mg): 2.06 Calc(mg): 35.8 Phos(mg): 362.67 Alch(mg): 0 Caff(mg): 0 Asp(mg): 0 Water(g): 119.69% of calories from fat: 52.84

APPLE CHICKEN SALAD

2 *cups cooked and diced Great Value Chicken Breast Fillets*
1 *cup sliced celery*
1/2 *cup sliced Great Value Black Olives*
3 *cups diced apples (unpeeled)*
1/2 *cup Great Value Mayonnaise*
1/4 *cup Great Value Sour Cream*
1/2 *teaspoon Great Value Lemon Juice*
1/8 *teaspoon curry (optional)*
Lettuce leaves
Apple slices to garnish

- Combine chicken, celery, olives and apples.
- Combine mayonnaise, sour cream, lemon juice and curry to make the dressing.
- Mix dressing with chicken and apple mixture. Toss to coat evenly.
- Serve on lettuce leaves and garnish with apple slices.
- Serves 6.

Total Calories: 319.84 Total Fat(g): 24.75 Sat. Fat(g): 0 Mono Fat(g): 7.54 Poly Fat(g): 12.65 Animal Fat(g): 6.15 Plant Fat(g): 18.44 Fish Fat(g): 0 Total Carb(g): 5.49 Comp. Carb(g): 3.89 Sugar(g): 1.6 Total Protein(g): 22.34 Anl Protein(g): 21.94 Plt Protein(g): 0.4 Fiber(g): 1.08 Chol(mg): 71.61 Sodium(mg): 269.52 Potm(mg): 305.64 Vitamin A: 37.9 Vitamin C(mg): 5.11 Iron(mg): 2.78 Calc(mg): 44.52 Phos(mg): 177.9 Alch(mg): 0 Caff(mg): 0 Asp(mg): 0 Water(g): 100.4 % of calories from fat: 69.64

DESSERT CHICKEN SALAD

2 1/2	*cups Great Value Chicken Breast Fillets*
1/2	*cup Great Value Raisins*
1/4	*cup Great Value Sour Cream*
1/4	*cup Great Value Mayonnaise*
3	*slices Great Value Pineapple, chopped*
1/4	*cup Great Value Apple Jelly*
	Sliced fruit of choice to garnish
	Sam's American Choice Sesame and Wheat Crackers

- Bake chicken breasts according to package directions; dice.
- Combine all ingredients in mixing bowl; stir thoroughly.
- Serve with crackers.
- Serves 4.

Total Calories: 387.95 Total Fat(g): 18.48 Sat. Fat(g): 0 Mono Fat(g): 6.55 Poly Fat(g): 8.66 Animal Fat(g): 6.67 Plant Fat(g): 11.69 Fish Fat(g): 0 Total Carb(g): 32.06 Comp. Carb(g): 17.5 Sugar(g): 14.56 Total Protein(g): 28.2 Anl Protein(g): 27.42 Plt Protein(g): 0.79 Fiber(g): 1.15 Chol(mg): 84.45 Sodium(mg): 150.94 Potm(mg): 416.73 Vitamin A: 30.5 Vitamin C(mg): 4.92 Iron(mg): 2.35 Calc(mg): 40.78 Phos(mg): 233.15 Alch(mg): 0 Caff(mg): 0 Asp(mg): 0 Water(g): 90.53 % of calories from fat: 42.87 (Nutritional information does not include crackers.)

SUPREME RICE AND TURKEY SALAD

- 2/3 cup Great Value Long Grain Rice
- 2 cups water
- 2 teaspoons Great Value Salt
- 2/3 cup Great Value Mayonnaise
- 1 tablespoon Great Value Lemon Juice
- 1/2 cup Great Value Milk
- 1/2 small Great Value Onion, chopped
- 2 1/2 cups cubed Great Value Cooked Turkey Breast
- 1 (8 ounce) can water chestnuts, sliced and drained
- 2 cups seedless purple grapes, halved
- 1 cup Great Value Cashews
- Great Value Salt and Pepper to taste
- Lemon or kiwi slices to garnish

- Wash rice thoroughly in warm water.
- In medium saucepan, combine rice, water and salt. Bring to a boil; cook over low heat for 45 minutes or until grains open and are tender and water is absorbed.
- In large bowl, combine mayonnaise, lemon juice, milk and onion.
- Stir in rice, turkey and water chestnuts; refrigerate until cold.
- Fold in grapes and cashews just before serving.
- Season to taste with salt and pepper.
- Spoon onto serving plate lined with lettuce leaves and garnish with lemon or kiwi slices.

Total Calories: 476.71 Total Fat(g): 35.97 Sat. Fat(g): 0 Mono Fat(g): 12.77 Poly Fat(g): 17.52 Animal Fat(g): 4.05 Plant Fat(g): 31.74 Fish Fat(g): 0 Total Carb(g): 30.26 Comp. Carb(g): 28 Sugar(g): 2.26 Total Protein(g): 15.86 Anl Protein(g): 7.95 Plt Protein(g): 7.91 Fiber(g): 3.17 Chol(mg): 29.14 Sodium(mg): 1733.91 Potm(mg): 379.53 Vitamin A: 13.02 Vitamin C(mg): 4.37 Iron(mg): 4.31 Calc(mg): 63.77 Phos(mg): 202.3 Alch(mg): 0 Caff(mg): 0 Asp(mg): 0 Water(g): 102.12 % of calories from fat: 67.91

TURKEY WALDORF SALAD

1	*can Great Value Chicken Broth*
1	*cup Great Value Long Grain Rice*
1	*cup Great Value Cooked Turkey Breast (cut into strips)*
3/4	*cup diced apple (unpeeled)*
1/2	*cup sliced celery*
2	*tablespoons slivered almonds, toasted*
3	*tablespoons poppy seed dressing*
	Great Value Leaf Spinach
	Radicchio

- Cook rice in chicken broth and allow to cool.
- Combine all ingredients, except leaf spinach and radicchio, in a medium bowl.
- Serve on spinach leaves and radicchio.
- Serves 2.

Total Calories: 489.73 Total Fat(g): 21.27 Sat. Fat(g): .7 Mono Fat(g): 5.45 Poly Fat(g): 3.22 Animal Fat(g): 5.66 Plant Fat(g): 4.86 Fish Fat(g): 0 Total Carb(g): 35.92 Comp. Carb(g): 31.42 Sugar(g): 4.5 Total Protein(g): 39.81 Anl Protein(g): 35.74 Plt Protein(g): 4.11 Fiber(g): 2.63 Chol(mg): 88.18 Sodium(mg): 1415.08 Potm(mg): 577.73 Vitamin A: 5.61 Vitamin C(mg): 3.87 Iron(mg): 3.63 Calc(mg): 84.29 Phos(mg): 341.06 Alch(mg): 0 Caff(mg): 0 Asp(mg): 0 Water(g): 203.46 % of calories from fat: 25.1

ORIENTAL MUSHROOM CHICKEN SALAD

- 2 *tablespoons slivered almonds, toasted*
- 12 *ounces Great Value Sliced Mushrooms*
- 1 *cup 1" cubes cooked Great Value Chicken Breast Tenderloins*
- 1 *cup Sam's American Choice Rice, cooked*
- 1/3 *cup diced Great Value Frozen Green Bell Pepper*
- 2 *tablespoons chopped Great Value Green Onion*
- *Lettuce leaves*

Dressing:

- 2/3 *cup Sam's American Choice Orange Juice*
- 1/3 *cup Great Value Vegetable Oil*
- 1/2 *teaspoon Great Value Salt*
- 1/4 *teaspoon ginger*
- 1/4 *teaspoon garlic powder*
- 1 *tablespoon soy sauce*
- 1 *tablespoon dry sherry*

- To toast almonds, place on a baking sheet in preheated 350-degree oven until light brown, approximately 5 minutes.
- Combine dressing ingredients; set aside.
- In a large bowl, combine chicken, rice, green pepper, almonds, green onion and mushrooms.
- Add reserved dressing and toss to mix.
- Cover and refrigerate at least 2 hours or overnight.
- Serve on bed of lettuce leaves.
- Serves 6.

Total Calories: 179.1 Total Fat(g): 5.07 Sat. Fat(g): 0 Mono Fat(g): 2.88 Poly Fat(g): 2.88 Animal Fat(g): 1.04 Plant Fat(g): 4.02 Fish Fat(g): 0 Total Carb(g): 23.49 Comp. Carb(g): 23.41 Sugar(g): 0.08 Total Protein(g): 12.19 Anl Protein(g): 9.01 Plt Protein(g): 3.18 Fiber(g): 1.27 Chol(mg): 24.83 Sodium(mg): 652.58 Potm(mg): 302.92 Vitamin A: 41.35 Vitamin C(mg): 18.74 Iron(mg): 1.66 Calc(mg): 28.45 Phos(mg): 141.82 Alch(mg): 0.38 Caff(mg): 0 Asp(mg): 0 Water(g): 83.51 % of calories from fat: 25.48

7-LAYER SALAD

1	*small head lettuce, shredded*
1/2	*cup sliced celery*
1/3	*cup chopped Great Value Frozen Onion*
1	*can Great Value Peas*
2	*cups Great Value Mayonnaise*
1/2	*cup grated Great Value Cheddar Cheese*
6	*slices Great Value Bacon*

- Layer lettuce, celery, onion and peas in a bowl.
- Spread mayonnaise completely on top, to sides of bowl.
- Cover with plastic wrap; let stand in refrigerator at least 6 hours or overnight.
- Fry bacon until crisp, then crumble.
- Just before serving, sprinkle cheese and bacon over salad.
- Serves 6.

Total Calories: 670.37 Total Fat(g): 70.12 Sat. Fat(g): 0 Mono Fat(g): 20.17 Poly Fat(g): 37.15 Animal Fat(g): 12.89 Plant Fat(g): 56.46 Fish Fat(g): 0 Total Carb(g): 12.33 Comp. Carb(g): 5.89 Sugar(g): 6.44 Total Protein(g): 8.18 Anl Protein(g): 5.8 Plt Protein(g): 2.38 Fiber(g): 2.81 Chol(mg): 47.1 Sodium(mg): 767.05 Potm(mg): 315.94 Vitamin A: 82.74 Vitamin C(mg): 12.78 Iron(mg): 6.4 Calc(mg): 104.13 Phos(mg): 138.18 Alch(mg): 0 Caff(mg): 0 Asp(mg): 0 Water(g): 134.55 % of calories from fat: 94.14

SUMMER SAUSAGE SALAD

6	*cups bite-size pieces Great Value Frozen Leaf Spinach, divided*
1	*small red onion, thinly sliced and halved*
1	*(16 ounce) can Great Value Lentil Beans, rinsed and drained*
14	*ounces Great Value Summer Sausage, thinly sliced*
1/3	*cup Great Value Italian Salad Dressing*

- In a salad bowl, layer four cups torn spinach, onion, beans, sausage, followed by remaining 2 cups torn spinach.
- To garnish top of salad, cut slices of sausage almost in half, then twist to make cartwheels.
- Drizzle dressing over salad.
- Serves 4.

Total Calories: 292.64 Total Fat(g): 13.78 Sat. Fat(g): 0 Mono Fat(g): 7.79 Poly Fat(g): 4.19 Animal Fat(g): 12.35 Plant Fat(g): 1.43 Fish Fat(g): 0 Total Carb(g): 27.03 Comp. Carb(g): 26.3 Sugar(g): 0.74 Total Protein(g): 17.35 Anl Protein(g): 6.88 Plt Protein(g): 10.47 Fiber(g): 10.43 Chol(mg): 38.46 Sodium(mg): 740.42 Potm(mg): 936.27 Vitamin A: 572.57 Vitamin C(mg): 25.92 Iron(mg): 5.22 Calc(mg): 117.82 Phos(mg): 234.24 Alch(mg): 0 Caff(mg): 0 Asp(mg): 0 Water(g): 162.58 % of calories from fat: 42.38

BACON, LETTUCE AND TOMATO SALAD

8	*slices Great Value Bacon*
3	*Great Value Tomatoes*
1/2	*medium head of lettuce*
1	*cup croutons*
1/2	*cup Great Value Mayonnaise or Salad Dressing*
	Great Value Salt and Pepper to taste

- Fry bacon until it is crisp, then crumble coarsely.
- Cut tomatoes into wedges.
- Add tomatoes and bacon to the remaining ingredients.
- Toss lightly.
- Season with salt and pepper to taste.
- Serves 4.

Total Calories: 352.46 Total Fat(g): 31.84 Sat. Fat(g): 0 Mono Fat(g): 10.52 Poly Fat(g): 14.89 Animal Fat(g): 8.31 Plant Fat(g): 23.34 Fish Fat(g): 0 Total Carb(g): 16.54 Comp. Carb(g): 12.29 Sugar(g): 4.25 Total Protein(g): 6.45 Anl Protein(g): 3.84 Plt Protein(g): 2.61 Fiber(g): 2.55 Chol(mg): 21.35 Sodium(mg): 1068.15 Potm(mg): 409.41 Vitamin A: 80.98 Vitamin C(mg): 26.91 Iron(mg): 3.57 Calc(mg): 32.67 Phos(mg): 96.56 Alch(mg): 0 Caff(mg): 0 Asp(mg): 0 Water(g): 155.04 % of calories from fat: 81.3

PACIFIC COAST HAM SALAD

- 3 cups wild rice, chilled
- 3 cups strips Great Value Cooked Turkey Ham, chilled
- 1 cup coarsely chopped Great Value Dry Roasted Peanuts
- 1/4 cup chopped Great Value Frozen Onion
- 1 cup cubed Great Value Pineapple Chunks, chilled
- 1 cup sliced Great Value Mushrooms
- 1 head lettuce
- 1 cup fresh raspberries
- 1 papaya, sliced

Dressing:

- 1/3 cup raspberry vinegar
- 1/3 cup olive oil
- 2 teaspoons Great Value Honey
- 1/4 teaspoon Great Value Salt

- Combine dressing ingredients in a jar; cover and shake well.
- Pour dressing over combined turkey ham, rice, peanuts, onion, pineapple and mushrooms. Toss lightly.
- Arrange lettuce leaves on a large serving platter or in a salad bowl.
- Top with turkey ham mixture.
- Arrange raspberries and papaya on top.
- Serves 6.

Total Calories: 424.71 Total Fat(g): 21.29 Sat. Fat(g): 0 Mono Fat(g): 9.1 Poly Fat(g): 8.79 Animal Fat(g): 4.71 Plant Fat(g): 16.58 Fish Fat(g): 0 Total Carb(g): 46.58 Comp. Carb(g): 38.63 Sugar(g): 7.95 Total Protein(g): 21.49 Anl Protein(g): 12.04 Plt Protein(g): 9.95 Fiber(g): 5.76 Chol(mg): 38.97 Sodium(mg): 1179.43 Potm(mg): 638.61 Vitamin A: 52.8 Vitamin C(mg): 44.38 Iron(mg): 2.62 Calc(mg): 45.84 Phos(mg): 340.1 Alch(mg): 0 Caff(mg): 0 Asp(mg): 0 Water(g): 147.75 % of calories from fat: 45.12

HAM AND VEGETABLE SALAD

- 1/2 *pound Great Value Elbow Macaroni*
- 2 *cups cooked and diced Great Value Ham*
- 1 *medium red bell pepper, chopped*
- 1 *medium yellow bell pepper, chopped*
- 1 *medium cucumber, seeded and chopped*
- 2 *cups sliced Great Value Mushrooms*
- 1 *cup sliced radishes*
- 1 *cup sliced Great Value Olives*
- 1/2 *cup chopped Great Value Onion*
- 3/4 *cup Great Value Italian Salad Dressing*
- 1 *clove garlic, crushed*
- 1 *cup grated Great Value Cheddar Cheese*

- Prepare elbow macaroni according to package directions; drain.
- In a medium bowl, combine all ingredients except cheese.
- Cover; chill thoroughly.
- Toss salad gently before serving.
- Top with cheese.
- Serves 6.

Total Calories: 584.23 Total Fat(g): 39.23 Sat. Fat(g): 0 Mono Fat(g): 16.16 Poly Fat(g): 3.82 Animal Fat(g): 32.06 Plant Fat(g): 5.69 Fish Fat(g): 0 Total Carb(g): 21.64 Comp. Carb(g): 21.45 Sugar(g): 0.19 Total Protein(g): 35.82 Anl Protein(g): 32.04 Plt Protein(g): 3.78 Fiber(g): 2.87 Chol(mg): 113.46 Sodium(mg): 1582.31 Potm(mg): 567.94 Vitamin A: 294.93 Vitamin C(mg): 40.53 Iron(mg): 2.77 Calc(mg): 505.82 Phos(mg): 563.78 Alch(mg): 0 Caff(mg): 0 Asp(mg): 0 Water(g): 220.28 % of calories from fat: 60.43

SAUSAGE AND BROCCOLI PASTA SALAD

1	*pound Great Value Cooked Smoked Sausage*
3 1/2	*cups Great Value Elbow Macaroni*
3	*cups chopped Great Value Frozen Broccoli*
4	*ounces Great Value Cheddar Cheese, julienned*
1/2	*cup sliced radishes*
1/2	*cup sliced Great Value Black Olives*

Dressing:

1/2	*cup Great Value Lemon Juice*
1/2	*cup Great Value Vegetable Oil*
1/4	*teaspoon dry mustard*
1/4	*teaspoon Great Value Salt*
1/4	*teaspoon garlic powder*
1/8	*teaspoon crushed red pepper*

- Cut sausage in 1/4" slices. Reserve half the slices for garnish.
- Cook macaroni according to package directions, omitting salt.
- Drain; rinse under cold water. Drain again.
- Blanch chopped broccoli in boiling water 2-3 minutes; rinse immediately under cold water.
- In large bowl, combine cooked macaroni, broccoli, half of sausage slices, cheese, radishes and black olives.
- In small bowl, blend dressing ingredients very well.
- Toss with macaroni mixture.
- Refrigerate 3-4 hours to blend flavors.
- Just before serving, use remaining sausage to garnish bowl, placing attractively around the edge in a spiral fashion.
- Serves 6.

Total Calories: 585.05 Total Fat(g): 30.65 Sat. Fat(g): 0 Mono Fat(g): 15.3 Poly Fat(g): 4.45 Animal Fat(g): 25.77 Plant Fat(g): 4.61 Fish Fat(g): 0 Total Carb(g): 54.85 Comp. Carb(g): 53.17 Sugar(g): 1.66 Total Protein(g): 23.82 Anl Protein(g): 12.95 Plt Protein(g): 10.88 Fiber(g): 5.46 Chol(mg): 65.98 Sodium(mg): 1393.5 Potm(mg): 391.04 Vitamin A: 220.02 Vitamin C(mg): 45.36 Iron(mg): 4.46 Calc(mg): 163.05 Phos(mg): 288.62 Alch(mg): 0 Caff(mg): 0 Asp(mg): 0 Water(g): 208.26 % of calories from fat: 47.15

SOUTHWESTERN HAM SALAD

- 2 cups sliced Great Value Cooked Ham
- 1 (16 ounce) can Great Value Red Kidney Beans, drained and rinsed
- 1 (16 ounce) can Great Value Sliced Black Olives, drained
- 1/2 cup chopped Great Value Frozen Onion
- 1/2 cup chopped Great Value Frozen Green Bell Pepper
- 1 large Great Value Tomato, peeled and chopped

Dressing:

- 2 teaspoons Great Value Sugar
- 1/2 cup Great Value Cider Vinegar
- 1/2 cup Great Value Vegetable Oil
- 1/2 teaspoon dry mustard
- 1/2 teaspoon cumin
- 1/2 teaspoon oregano
- 1/2 teaspoon Great Value Salt
- 2 tablespoons chopped parsley

- Mix ham, beans, olives, onion, green pepper and tomato in large bowl.
- Combine dressing ingredients in a jar; shake to mix.
- Pour over ham mixture, toss and refrigerate several hours. Stir occasionally.
- Serves 6.

Total Calories: 170.21 Total Fat(g): 5.48 Sat. Fat(g): 0 Mono Fat(g): 4.1 Poly Fat(g): 2.98 Animal Fat(g): 1.82 Plant Fat(g): 3.87 Fish Fat(g): 0 Total Carb(g): 18.72 Comp. Carb(g): 17.09 Sugar(g): 1.63 Total Protein(g): 12.76 Anl Protein(g): 7.69 Plt Protein(g): 5.07 Fiber(g): 6.65 Chol(mg): 22.26 Sodium(mg): 1365.07 Potm(mg): 428.51 Vitamin A: 26.59 Vitamin C(mg): 11.83 Iron(mg): 2.03 Calc(mg): 45.77 Phos(mg): 210.48 Alch(mg): 0 Caff(mg): 0 Asp(mg): 0 Water(g): 106.31 % of calories from fat: 28.98

HEARTY POLISH SAUSAGE SUPPER SALAD

4	*Great Value Red Potatoes*
1	*(16 ounce) package Great Value Green Peas*
1/4	*cup chopped Great Value Frozen Onion*
1	*(8 ounce) can sauerkraut, rinsed and drained*
3/4	*cup diced celery*
1/2	*cup grated Great Value Mozzarella Cheese*
1	*cup Great Value Mayonnaise*
2	*tablespoons Great Value Brown Mustard*
1	*teaspoon crushed caraway*
1/2	*teaspoon garlic salt*
1/8	*teaspoon Great Value Pepper*
1	*pound Great Value Cooked Polish Sausage*

- Cook potatoes and set aside.
- Cook green peas as directed on package, omitting butter and increasing water to 3 tablespoons; drain.
- In a large bowl, combine peas, potatoes, sauerkraut, celery, onion and cheese; toss lightly to mix.
- In a small bowl, combine mayonnaise, mustard, caraway, garlic salt and pepper; mix well.
- Add to potato mixture; mix gently.
- Chill about 2 hours.
- Spoon salad in center of a serving platter and arrange Polish sausage around it.
- Serves 7.

Total Calories: 677.94 Total Fat(g): 57.92 Sat. Fat(g): 0 Mono Fat(g): 22.18 Poly Fat(g): 19.81 Animal Fat(g): 32.25 Plant Fat(g): 25.44 Fish Fat(g): 0 Total Carb(g): 23.98 Comp. Carb(g): 20.14 Sugar(g): 3.84 Total Protein(g): 21.33 Anl Protein(g): 16.07 Plt Protein(g): 5.26 Fiber(g): 6.47 Chol(mg): 88.65 Sodium(mg): 1713.62 Potm(mg): 681.65 Vitamin A: 171.95 Vitamin C(mg): 36.2 Iron(mg): 6.43 Calc(mg): 156.32 Phos(mg): 274.65 Alch(mg): 0 Caff(mg): 0 Asp(mg): 0 Water(g): 185.34 % of calories from fat: 76.89

SUMMER SALAD STROGANOFF

1 cup Great Value Sour Cream
2 tablespoons Great Value Brown Mustard
2 tablespoons Great Value Lemon Juice
8 ounces Sam's American Choice Beef Patties, broiled and cut into 1" squares
8 ounces Great Value mushrooms, sliced
1 medium onion, thinly sliced and separated into rings
Great Value Salt and Pepper to taste
Lettuce leaves
Chopped parsley to garnish

- In bowl, mix together sour cream, mustard and lemon juice.
- Toss beef, mushrooms and onion rings with sour cream mixture. Season with salt and pepper to taste.
- Cover; chill several hours or overnight.
- Serve on a bed of lettuce leaves; garnish with parsley.
- Serves 4.

Total Calories: 335.01 Total Fat(g): 18.47 Sat. Fat(g): 0 Mono Fat(g): 8.09 Poly Fat(g): 2.25 Animal Fat(g): 12.88 Plant Fat(g): 4.8 Fish Fat(g): 0 Total Carb(g): 11.09 Comp. Carb(g): 10.67 Sugar(g): 0.44 Total Protein(g): 31.11 Anl Protein(g): 28.76 Plt Protein(g): 2.35 Fiber(g): 3.45 Chol(mg): 91.51 Sodium(mg): 440.84 Potm(mg): 605.28 Vitamin A: 269.07 Vitamin C(mg): 52.2 Iron(mg): 2.16 Calc(mg): 309.67 Phos(mg): 379.98 Alch(mg): 0 Caff(mg): 0 Asp(mg): 0 Water(g): 280.56 % of calories from fat: 49.62

SPEEDY RANCHERO SALAD

1	*cup Great Value Salsa*
2	*green onions with tops, thinly sliced*
1/4	*cup chopped fresh cilantro*
1/4	*cup Great Value Vegetable Oil*
1	*teaspoon Great Value Lemon Juice*
1	*clove garlic, minced*
1/2	*teaspoon Great Value Salt*
1	*(15 ounce) can Great Value Pinto Beans, drained*
1 1/2	*cups diced Great Value Tomatoes*
1	*ripe avocado, peeled, seeded and diced*
1	*pound Great Value Beef Patties, broiled*
	Great Value Salt and Pepper
	Sam's American Choice Tortilla Chips

- Combine first 7 ingredients; mix well.
- Toss beans with 1/4 cup of the salsa mixture; chill.
- Toss tomatoes and avocado with 1/4 cup of the salsa mixture; chill.
- Sprinkle meat with salt and pepper; broil according to package directions; cut into small squares.
- Toss meat with 1/4 cup of the salsa mixture; arrange on a platter.
- Arrange beans, tomato mixture and meat on greens.
- Serve with tortilla chips.
- Serves 6.

Total Calories: 357.19 Total Fat(g): 21.86 Sat. Fat(g): 0 Mono Fat(g): 11.34 Poly Fat(g): 2.41 Animal Fat(g): 14.12 Plant Fat(g): 7.73 Fish Fat(g): 0 Total Carb(g): 20.03 Comp. Carb(g): 19.78 Sugar(g): 0.25 Total Protein(g): 24.2 Anl Protein(g): 18.89Plt Protein(g): 5.32 Fiber(g): 6.27 Chol(mg): 66.48 Sodium(mg): 992.8 Potm(mg): 881.12 Vitamin A: 178.87 Vitamin C(mg): 15.03 Iron(mg): 4.01 Calc(mg): 54.24 Phos(mg): 235.88 Alch(mg): 0 Caff(mg): 0 Asp(mg): 0 Water(g): 184.81% of calories from fat: 55.08 (Nutritional information does not include tortilla chips.)

CHILI SALAD

- *Shredded leaf spinach*
- 1 *bowl chili (see accompanying recipe, "Ranch Style Chili")*
- 1 1/2 *cups diced Great Value Tomatoes*
- 1/2 *cup chopped Great Value Frozen Onion*
- 1/2 *cup sliced Great Value Green Olives*
- 1 *avocado, sliced*
- 1 *cup grated Great Value Cheddar Cheese*
- *Sam's American Choice Tortilla Chips*

- On individual plates, place spinach leaves; spoon hot chili on lettuce.
- Top with tomatoes, onion, olives, avocado and cheese, in that order.
- Serve with tortilla chips.
- Serves 6.

RANCH STYLE CHILI

- 1 *pound ground beef*
- 1/2 *cup chopped Great Value Frozen Onion*
- 2 *teaspoons Great Value Corn Oil*
- 4 *ounces Great Value Tomato Sauce*
- 2 *cups water*
- 3 *tablespoons Great Value Chili Seasoning (vary to taste)*
- 1 *teaspoon paprika*
- 1/2 *teaspoon Great Value Salt*
- *Red pepper*
- 1 *clove garlic*
- 1 *teaspoon cumin*
- 1 *(14.5 ounce) can Great Value Tomatoes, chopped*
- 1 *teaspoon Great Value Flour*
- 2 *tablespoons warm water*

- Add the ground beef and onion to the oil, cooking over medium heat until meat is brown.
- Add the remaining ingredients, cover and simmer about 1 hour. Stir occasionally while cooking.
- Correct seasonings to taste. Thicken with flour mixed with warm water.
- Use 1 recipe *Ranch Style Chili* in *Chili Salad*.

Total Calories: 592.19 Total Fat(g): 45.62 Sat. Fat(g): 0 Mono Fat(g): 17.95 Poly Fat(g): 5.56 Animal Fat(g): 33.33 Plant Fat(g): 10.94 Fish Fat(g): 0 Total Carb(g): 17.16 Comp. Carb(g): 17.03 Sugar(g): 0.13 Total Protein(g): 31.59 Anl Protein(g): 27.66 Plt Protein(g): 3.96 Fiber(g): 4.86 Chol(mg): 117.26 Sodium(mg): 948.94 Potm(mg): 1012.18 Vitamin A: 325.03 Vitamin C(mg): 31.96 Iron(mg): 3.48 Calc(mg): 462.92 Phos(mg): 478.25 Alch(mg): 0 Caff(mg): 0 Asp(mg): 0 Water(g): 345.83 % of calories from fat: 69.33 (Nutritional information does not include tortilla chips.)

WILTED SPINACH BEEF SALAD

2	*pounds Sam's American Choice Frozen Beef Patties, broiled*
3	*tablespoons olive oil*
1/2	*cup finely sliced Great Value Frozen Onion*
2	*cloves garlic, finely minced*
2	*tablespoons teriyaki sauce*
2	*tablespoons sherry*
1	*teaspoon Sam's American Choice Dijon Mustard*
1	*teaspoon horseradish*
1/2	*teaspoon dill weed*
	Great Value Salt and Pepper to taste
5	*cups bite-size pieces Great Value Frozen Leaf Spinach, cleaned and stems removed*
1	*medium red onion, thinly sliced*
1	*cup grated Great Value Monterey Jack Cheese*
8	*Great Value Whole Tomatoes, halved*

- Press beef into patties (1/8" thick) and broil according to package directions.
- Heat olive oil in large frying pan over medium heat; add onion and garlic and fry 1-2 minutes.
- Add quartered beef patties; stir-fry over high heat 2-3 minutes.
- Mix together teriyaki sauce, sherry, mustard, horseradish and dill weed. Add to beef in skillet; cook 1 minute. Season with salt and pepper to taste.
- In large salad bowl, place spinach, onion, cheese and tomatoes.
- Pour warm beef and sauce over spinach mixture. Toss to coat.
- Serve immediately.
- Serves 6.

Total Calories: 700.63 Total Fat(g): 51.53 Sat. Fat(g): 0 Mono Fat(g): 24.74 Poly Fat(g): 3.5 Animal Fat(g): 43.04 Plant Fat(g): 8.49 Fish Fat(g): 0 Total Carb(g): 18.56 Comp. Carb(g): 17 Sugar(g): 1.55 Total Protein(g): 42.14 Anl Protein(g): 36.17 Plt Protein(g): 5.98 Fiber(g): 6.63 Chol(mg): 148.03 Sodium(mg): 1421.3 Potm(mg): 1312.72 Vitamin A: 1219.66 Vitamin C(mg): 66.34 Iron(mg): 7.45 Calc(mg): 460.67 Phos(mg): 484.55 Alch(mg): 0.93 Caff(mg): 0 Asp(mg): 0 Water(g): 416.47 % of calories from fat: 66.19

HOT GRILLED APPLE SALAD

2	*cups cored and thinly sliced apples*
3	*cups shredded red cabbage*
4	*teaspoons Great Value Butter, cut up*
3	*tablespoons red wine vinegar*
4	*teaspoons Great Value Sugar*
3/4	*teaspoon Great Value Salt*
1/4	*teaspoon caraway seed*
1/4	*teaspoon Great Value Pepper*

- In a bowl, toss all ingredients.
- Turn out onto 24" x 18" piece of heavy duty foil.
- Fold edges around apple mixture and seal edges tightly.
- Grill packet, on covered grill, over medium-hot briquets 45 minutes or until apples are tender, turning packet every 15 minutes.
- Serves 4.

Total Calories: 95.5 Total Fat(g): 4.48 Sat. Fat(g): 0 Mono Fat(g): 3.28 Poly Fat(g): 1.37 Animal Fat(g): 4.15 Plant Fat(g): 0.33 Fish Fat(g): 0 Total Carb(g): 15.2 Comp. Carb(g): 10.96 Sugar(g): 4.24 Total Protein(g): 1.64 Anl Protein(g): 1 Plt Protein(g): 0.64 Fiber(g): 1.86 Chol(mg): 11.03 Sodium(mg): 483.17 Potm(mg): 148.45 Vitamin A: 41.88 Vitamin C(mg): 22.92 Iron(mg): 0.85 Calc(mg): 24.81 Phos(mg): 21.87 Alch(mg): 0 Caff(mg): 0 Asp(mg): 0 Water(g): 80.27 % of calories from fat: 42.22

SUMMER FRUIT SALAD

2	*cups cooked Great Value Rice, cooled to room temperature*
1/2	*cup quartered strawberries*
1/2	*cup quartered Great Value Pear Halves*
1/2	*cup quartered Great Value Peach Halves*
1/2	*cup halved Great Value Chunk Pineapples (reserve juice)*
1/2	*cup banana slices*
1/4	*cup juice from Great Value Pineapple Chunks*
2	*tablespoons Great Value Plain Yogurt*
1	*tablespoon Great Value Honey*
	Leaf spinach or mint

- Combine rice and fruits in large bowl.
- Blend pineapple juice, yogurt and honey in small bowl; pour over rice mixture. Toss lightly.
- Serve on baby spinach or garnish with mint.
- Serves 4.

Total Calories: 188.04 Total Fat(g): 0.98 Sat. Fat(g): 0 Mono Fat(g): 0.95 Poly Fat(g): 1.16 Animal Fat(g): 0.22 Plant Fat(g): 0.76 Fish Fat(g): 0 Total Carb(g): 42.72 Comp. Carb(g): 38.35 Sugar(g): 4.38 Total Protein(g): 3.93 Anl Protein(g): 0.75 Plt Protein(g): 3.18 Fiber(g): 2.63 Chol(mg): 0.87 Sodium(mg): 341.54 Potm(mg): 347.22 Vitamin A: 113.77 Vitamin C(mg): 19.3 Iron(mg): 1.71 Calc(mg): 68.78 Phos(mg): 118.68 Alch(mg): 0 Caff(mg): 0 Asp(mg): 0 Water(g): 154.89 % of calories from fat: 4.69

FRESH PINEAPPLE COLE SLAW

1	*small head cabbage, shredded*
1	*(20 ounce) can Great Value Pineapple Chunks, reserve juice*
1/2	*cup Great Value Raisins*
1/4	*cup chopped Great Value Dry Roasted Peanuts*

Dressing:

1/4	*cup Great Value Vegetable Oil*
	Juice from pineapple
1	*tablespoon Great Value Lemon Juice*
2	*tablespoons Great Value Honey*
1	*tablespoon toasted sesame seeds*

- In a jar with lid, make dressing by combining oil, juice from can of pineapple chunks, lemon juice, honey and sesame seeds; shake well.
- In a large bowl, combine cabbage, pineapple chunks, raisins and dressing; chill.
- To serve, add chopped nuts; toss gently.
- Serves 6.

Total Calories: 224.94 Total Fat(g): 5.7 Sat. Fat(g): 0 Mono Fat(g): 4.48 Poly Fat(g): 3.74 Animal Fat(g): 0 Plant Fat(g): 5.7 Fish Fat(g): 0 Total Carb(g): 47 Comp. Carb(g): 41.16 Sugar(g): 5.84 Total Protein(g): 4.09 Anl Protein(g): 0 Plt Protein(g): 4.09 Fiber(g): 3.48 Chol(mg): 0 Sodium(mg): 79.4 Potm(mg): 489.73 Vitamin A: 14.34 Vitamin C(mg): 16.03 Iron(mg): 1.38 Calc(mg): 53.02 Phos(mg): 216.31 Alch(mg): 0 Caff(mg): 0 Asp(mg): 0 Water(g): 40.55 % of calories from fat: 22.81

SUMMER LIGHT SALAD

2	*cups boiling water*
1	*(3 ounce) package lemon gelatin*
1	*(3 ounce) package lime gelatin*
1	*can Great Value Evaporated Milk*
1	*cup Great Value Lite Mayonnaise*
1	*cup Great Value Lowfat Cottage Cheese*
1	*(20 ounce) can Great Value Crushed Pineapple, leave in own juice*
3/4	*cup Great Value Dry Roasted Peanuts*
2	*apples, grated*

- Use 1 cup boiling water to dissolve each flavor of gelatin.
- Mix in remaining ingredients and refrigerate overnight or until set (5-6 hours).
- Serves 10.

Total Calories: 233.78 Total Fat(g): 15.39 Sat. Fat(g): 0 Mono Fat(g): 5.47 Poly Fat(g): 7.38 Animal Fat(g): 1.21 Plant Fat(g): 14.16 Fish Fat(g): 0 Total Carb(g): 20.92 Comp. Carb(g): 17.41 Sugar(g): 3.52 Total Protein(g): 8.27 Anl Protein(g): 5.04 Plt Protein(g): 3.23 Fiber(g): 2.19 Chol(mg): 3.98 Sodium(mg): 361.11 Potm(mg): 253.03 Vitamin A: 9.9 Vitamin C(mg): 5.42 Iron(mg): 2.43 Calc(mg): 55.84 Phos(mg): 90.91 Alch(mg): 0 Caff(mg): 0 Asp(mg): 0 Water(g): 28.34 % of calories from fat: 59.25

HONEYED GRAPEFRUIT SALAD

- 2 *Ruby Red grapefruits, sectioned*
- 2 *oranges, sectioned*
- 1 *pint strawberries, washed and hulled*
- 2 *medium avocados, peeled, pitted and sliced*
- 1 *banana, peeled and sliced*
- 1/2 *cantaloupe or honeydew melon, peeled and cut into bite-size pieces*

Dressing:

- 2/3 *cup Great Value Vegetable Oil*
- 1 *teaspoon grated grapefruit peel*
- 1/3 *cup Great Value Pink Grapefruit Juice*
- 2 *tablespoons Great Value Lemon Juice*
- 2 *tablespoons Great Value Honey*
- 1/2 *teaspoon paprika*
- 1/2 *teaspoon Great Value Salt*

- To make dressing, combine all ingredients in a jar with lid, shake well and chill.
- Arrange fruit in a large salad bowl or on individual salad plates.
- Shake chilled salad dressing vigorously; pour on salad before serving.
- Serves 6.

Total Calories: 476.71 Total Fat(g): 35.97 Sat. Fat(g): 0 Mono Fat(g): 12.77 Poly Fat(g): 17.52 Animal Fat(g): 4.05 Plant Fat(g): 31.74 Fish Fat(g): 0 Total Carb(g): 30.26 Comp. Carb(g): 28 Sugar(g): 2.26 Total Protein(g): 15.86 Anl Protein(g): 7.95 Plt Protein(g): 7.91 Fiber(g): 3.17 Chol(mg): 29.14 Sodium(mg): 1733.91 Potm(mg): 379.53 Vitamin A: 13.02 Vitamin C(mg): 4.37 Iron(mg): 4.31 Calc(mg): 63.77 Phos(mg): 202.3 Alch(mg): 0 Caff(mg): 0 Asp(mg): 0 Water(g): 102.12 % of calories from fat: 67.91

DAISY HAWAIIAN AMBROSIA

- 1 cup Great Value Crushed Pineapple, drained
- 1 1/2 cups Great Value Mandarin Oranges, well drained
- 1 cup Great Value Miniature Marshmallows
- 3/4 cup Great Value Flaked Coconut
- 1 small jar Great Value Maraschino Cherries, drained
- 1 cup Great Value Sour Cream
- 1/2 cup walnuts or almonds

- Mix all ingredients together and place in a lightly greased mold or in a bowl. Chill overnight.

- Serves as a salad, entrée, accompaniment or dessert.

- Serves 6.

Variation:

- Great Value Sliced Pears or Peaches may be substituted in whole or in part for maraschino cherries.

Total Calories: 282.17 Total Fat(g): 23.24 Sat. Fat(g): 0 Mono Fat(g): 4.31 Poly Fat(g): 6.09 Animal Fat(g): 6.75 Plant Fat(g): 16.49 Fish Fat(g): 0 Total Carb(g): 33.7 Comp. Carb(g): 17.28 Sugar(g): 15.76 Total Protein(g): 11.45 Anl Protein(g): 1.08 Plt Protein(g): 10.37 Fiber(g): 1.83 Chol(mg): 14.44 Sodium(mg): 43.28 Potm(mg): 260.13 Vitamin A: 105.45 Vitamin C(mg): 10.26 Iron(mg): 1.02 Calc(mg): 59.78 Phos(mg): 97.36 Alch(mg): 0 Caff(mg): 0 Asp(mg): 0 Water(g): 45.88 % of calories from fat: 74.13

CRANBERRY WALNUT SALAD

- 3/4 *cup chopped walnuts*
- 1 *cup coarsely chopped cranberries (uncooked)*
- 1/4 *cup Great Value Sugar*
- 2 *(3 ounce) packages lemon gelatin*
- 1 3/4 *cups boiling water*
- 3 *tablespoons Great Value Lemon Juice*
- 1/4 *teaspoon Great Value Salt*
- 8 *ounces Great Value Pineapple Chunks, with syrup*
- 10 *ounces Sam's American Choice Lemon Lime Drink*
- 8 *ounces Great Value Cream Cheese, softened*
- *Great Value Leaf Spinach*

- Toast walnuts at 300 degrees 10 minutes; set aside.
- Mix cranberries with sugar. Let stand while preparing salad.
- Dissolve gelatin in boiling water. Stir in lemon juice and salt.
- Drain syrup from pineapple into gelatin mixture. Cool thoroughly.
- Stir in lemon lime drink. Cool until thickened.
- Set aside 1 1/2 cups of gelatin mixture for cream cheese.
- Stir cranberries, pineapple and half of walnuts into remaining clear gelatin. Spoon into 6-cup mold; chill.
- Meanwhile, blend cream cheese into reserve gelatin. Stir in walnuts.
- When fruit layer is almost set, carefully spoon creamy mixture on top.
- Chill several hours or overnight until firm.
- Unmold onto spinach leaves to serve.
- Serves 8.

Total Calories: 179.1 Total Fat(g): 5.07 Sat. Fat(g): 0 Mono Fat(g): 2.88 Poly Fat(g): 2.88 Animal Fat(g): 1.04 Plant Fat(g): 4.02 Fish Fat(g): 0 Total Carb(g): 23.49 Comp. Carb(g): 23.41 Sugar(g): 0.08 Total Protein(g): 12.19 Anl Protein(g): 9.01 Plt Protein(g): 3.18 Fiber(g): 1.27 Chol(mg): 24.83 Sodium(mg): 652.58 Potm(mg): 302.92 Vitamin A: 41.35 Vitamin C(mg): 18.74 Iron(mg): 1.66 Calc(mg): 28.45 Phos(mg): 141.82 Alch(mg): 0.38 Caff(mg): 0 Asp(mg): 0 Water(g): 83.51 % of calories from fat: 25.48

PEACHY SURPRISE SALAD

- 3/4 cup melted Great Value Butter
- 2 1/4 cups crushed Great Value Pretzel Sticks
- 1 3/4 cups Great Value Sugar, divided
- 1 (8 ounce) package Great Value Cream Cheese, softened
- 1 (8 ounce) carton Great Value Whipped Topping
- 3 cups Great Value Sliced Peaches (with juice)
- 1 (16 ounce) can Great Value Pineapple Chunks (with juice)
- 1 (6 ounce) package peach gelatin
- 2 cups ice
- Pecans to garnish

- Combine butter, pretzels and 1/4 cup sugar in 13" x 9" pan, mixing and spreading over bottom of pan.
- Blend cream cheese, whipped topping and 1 1/2 cups sugar in a bowl. Spread over pretzel layer.
- Drain juices from peaches and pineapples, reserving juices.
- Combine juices with enough water to measure 2 cups and heat to boiling.
- Dissolve gelatin in hot juice mixture.
- Stir in 2 cups ice and chill until thickened.
- Fold in fruit. Spread over cream cheese mixture.
- Garnish with pecans.
- Serves 8.

Total Calories: 626.45 Total Fat(g): 40.65 Sat. Fat(g): 0 Mono Fat(g): 13.44 Poly Fat(g): 0 Animal Fat(g): 36.38 Plant Fat(g): 4.26 Fish Fat(g): 0 Total Carb(g): 66.14 Comp. Carb(g): 19.83 Sugar(g): 46.33 Total Protein(g): 9.89 Anl Protein(g): 8.85 Plt Protein(g): 1.04 Fiber(g): 1.13 Chol(mg): 104.58 Sodium(mg): 377.86 Potm(mg): 259.82 Vitamin A: 458.23 Vitamin C(mg): 4.31 Iron(mg): 2.03 Calc(mg): 63.64 Phos(mg): 179.71 Alch(mg): 0 Caff(mg): 0 Asp(mg): 0 Water(g): 27.39 % of calories from fat: 58.40